"Sidney Greidanus poured a lifetime of preaching Christ from the entire Bible and teaching others to do so into this guided tour of Scripture's unfolding history of creation, redemption, and consummation. With brevity and clarity, he shows our beauty-creating God at work, bringing order to the 'formless and void' deep. Then, when Satanic lies and human rebellion injected chaos, disorder, desolation, and death, the Lord executed his eternal plan to redeem and reorder his creation through Jesus Christ. This study is full of God's Word, set into context by Greidanus's insightful comment. It offers fresh and ancient perspectives on Scripture's unity and its central focus: Christ the Redeemer."

Dennis E. Johnson, Professor Emeritus of Practical Theology, Westminster Seminary California; author, *Him We Proclaim*; *Walking with Jesus through His Word*; and *Journeys with Jesus*

T0334679

From Chaos to Cosmos

Short Studies in Biblical Theology

Edited by Dane C. Ortlund and Miles V. Van Pelt

From Chaos to Cosmos

Creation to New Creation

Sidney Greidanus

WHEATON, ILLINOIS

Library of Congress Cataloging-in-Publication Data

Names: Greidanus, Sidney, 1935– author. | Ortlund, Dane Calvin, editor. | Van Pelt, Miles V., 1969– editor.
Title: From chaos to cosmos: creation to new creation / Sidney Greidanus, Dane C. Ortlund and Miles V. Van Pelt, series editors.
Description: Wheaton, Illinois: Crossway, [2018] | Series: Short studies in biblical theology | Includes bibliographical references and index.
Identifiers: LCCN 2018016920 (print) | LCCN 2018035748 (ebook) | ISBN 9781433554988 (pdf) | ISBN 9781433554995 (mobi) | ISBN 9781433555008 (epub) | ISBN 9781433554971 (tp) | ISBN 9781433555008 (ePub) | ISBN 9781433554995 (Mobipocket)
Subjects: LCSH: Biblical cosmology—Textbooks. | Cosmogony—Textbooks. | Bible—Theology—Textbooks.
Classification: LCC BS651 (ebook) | LCC BS651 .G794 2018 (print) | DDC 231.7/65—dc23
LC record available at https://lccn.loc.gov/2018016920

This book is dedicated to the memory of
my parents, Nies and Sjoukje Greidanus (née Tiersma),
and my parents-in-law,
Lambert and Reingje Visscher (née Breman).

"Blessed are the dead who die in the Lord from now on."
"Blessed indeed," says the Spirit, "that they may rest from their labors,
for their deeds follow them!"
Revelation 14:13

Contents

List of Abbreviations

BA	*The Biblical Archaeologist*
BSac	*Bibliotheca Sacra*
CTJ	*Calvin Theological Journal*
MT	Masoretic Text of the Hebrew Old Testament
LXX	Septuagint
TDOT	*Theological Dictionary of the Old Testament*
TynBul	*Tyndale Bulletin*
VT	*Vetus Testamentum*
WeslTJ	*Wesleyan Theological Journal*

Series Preface

Most of us tend to approach the Bible early on in our Christian lives as a vast, cavernous, and largely impenetrable book. We read the text piecemeal, finding golden nuggets of inspiration here and there, but remain unable to plug any given text meaningfully into the overarching storyline. Yet one of the great advances in evangelical biblical scholarship over the past few generations has been the recovery of biblical theology—that is, a renewed appreciation for the Bible as a theologically unified, historically rooted, progressively unfolding, and ultimately Christ-centered narrative of God's covenantal work in our world to redeem sinful humanity.

This renaissance of biblical theology is a blessing, yet little of it has been made available to the general Christian population. The purpose of Short Studies in Biblical Theology is to connect the resurgence of biblical theology at the academic level with everyday believers. Each volume is written by a capable scholar or churchman who is consciously writing in a way that requires no prerequisite theological training of the reader. Instead, any thoughtful Christian disciple can track with and benefit from these books.

Each volume in this series takes a whole-Bible theme and traces it through Scripture. In this way readers not only learn about a given theme but also are given a model for how to read the Bible as a coherent whole.

We have launched this series because we love the Bible, we love the church, and we long for the renewal of biblical theology in the academy to enliven the hearts and minds of Christ's disciples all around the world. As editors, we have found few discoveries more thrilling in life than that of seeing the whole Bible as a unified story of God's gracious acts of redemption, and indeed of seeing the whole Bible as ultimately about Jesus, as he himself testified (Luke 24:27; John 5:39).

The ultimate goal of Short Studies in Biblical Theology is to magnify the Savior and to build up his church—magnifying the Savior through showing how the whole Bible points to him and his gracious rescue of helpless sinners; and building up the church by strengthening believers in their grasp of these life-giving truths.

Dane C. Ortlund and Miles V. Van Pelt

Preface

Studying the chaos–cosmos theme from Genesis 1 to Revelation 22 is a fascinating journey. It deepens our understanding of the original creation and the coming new creation. It helps us see not only the unity of the Scriptures but also the centrality of Christ in the Scriptures. The chaos–cosmos theme makes us aware of the various forms of chaos caused by the fall into sin and God's cursing the ground: pain, suffering, enmity, violence, enslavement, and death. But it also makes us aware of God's sovereignty over chaos: his turning chaos into cosmos (or micro-cosmos) merely by speaking, his grace for his fallen creatures, his aim to deliver them, his faithfulness to his covenant promises, and, by making ever new starts, his intent to restore his creation to the cosmos he intended it to be in the beginning.

In this book I quote Scripture extensively, sometimes providing quick explanations in square brackets. I have inserted italics in biblical quotations to emphasize words and phrases important for our topic. In the footnotes I provide more detailed explanations, references, and parallel passages. Articles, essays, and books that are not listed in the select bibliography are referenced in the footnotes. For the sake of consistency, the pointing in all Hebrew and Greek transliterations (also in quotations) have been upgraded to the latest *SBL* standards.

May this book help many preachers, teachers, churches, study groups, and individuals to discern the unity of Scripture and the centrality of Christ as we trace the chaos–cosmos theme along the biblical storyline of creation, fall, redemption, and new creation.

———

I thank Drs. Dane Ortlund and Miles Van Pelt for inviting me to contribute to the Short Studies in Biblical Theology series, for reserving for me the chaos–cosmos theme which really piqued my interest, and for skillfully editing this contribution. I have thoroughly enjoyed this journey. I also thank the staff of Crossway, especially editor Tara Davis, for competently guiding this book to publication.

I am grateful to my proofreaders, the Rev. Ryan Faber, my former student at Calvin Theological Seminary, and the late Dr. Howard Vanderwell, my former colleague, for their questions, suggestions, and corrections. I thank our local Bible study leader Jan Lanser for her forthright answer when I asked her if she could use this book for her Bible study groups. "Only if it has discussion questions!" was her honest reply. This response led to the inclusion of questions after each of the fourteen lessons—making this book much more user-friendly for both individual and Bible study groups. I also express my appreciation to the staff of the library of Calvin College and Calvin Theological Seminary for their helpful service.

Again I thank my wife, Marie, for taking care of many of the household chores so that I was able to concentrate on the research and writing of this book. Finally, I am grateful to the Lord for providing me, even in old age, with health, strength, and surprising insights during the writing of this book.

1

The Chaos–Cosmos Theme in Genesis, Exodus, and Joshua[1]

The chaos–cosmos theme falls under the overarching biblical theme of God's kingship and God's coming kingdom. It is also a subset of the biblical storyline of creation, fall, redemption, new creation.

Some biblical scholars prefer not to use the word *chaos* because the Hebrew does not use *chaos* but rather several other words, such as *without form, void, darkness, the deep, the waters, the seas, Rahab, great sea creatures,* and *Leviathan,* and because scholars use *chaos* in many different senses, some assuming that chaos is inherently evil.[2] We can still use this common term, however, if we define it correctly. Among several options, *Webster's Unabridged Dictionary* offers a good, initial definition of *chaos*: "The infinity of space or formless matter supposed to have preceded the existence of the

---

1. Genesis, Exodus, and Joshua are the historical books in which chaos ("darkness," "the deep," "the waters," "the flood," "the sea," "the Jordan") plays a major role.

2. See, for example, Eric Vail, *Creation and Chaos Talk,* 16–25, 77–154, 210–13; John Walton, *Genesis 1 as Ancient Cosmology,* 27–28; and Rebecca Watson, *Chaos Uncreated,* 1–3,13–19. Watson states, "Any attempt to translate this vocabulary in terms of 'chaos' would require careful definition, and is best avoided" (16).

ordered universe." *Webster's* also offers us a workable definition for *cosmos*: "The world or universe regarded as an orderly, harmonious system."

Starting out with these rather general definitions of *chaos* and *cosmos*, we can add the more specific forms of chaos and cosmos as we move through the Scriptures from Genesis 1 to Revelation 22. Genesis 1 begins with, "In the beginning, God created the heavens and the earth"—an orderly, harmonious universe.[3] Revelation 21 and 22 describe "a new heaven and a new earth" (Rev. 21:1)—another orderly, harmonious universe. Between these cosmic bookends (called *inclusio*) we find microcosmic units of disorder and restored order—units such as the earth, the animal kingdom, humanity, nations, and individuals. All of these ordered microcosmic units prefigure the end-time orderly cosmos described in Revelation.[4]

The Ancient Near Eastern Background

We must understand the biblical chaos–cosmos theme against the broader background of the ancient world, in which chaos was associated with the sea, the waters. Israel shared with its ancient Near Eastern neighbors the worldview of a three-storied universe. John Day explains: "All those passages in the Old Testament which speak about God's control of the sea at the time of creation naturally presuppose the archaic worldview shared by the ancient Israelites along with other peoples of the ancient Near East that both above the domed firmament of heaven and below the earth there is a cosmic sea. Rain was regarded as having its origin in the cosmic

---

3. Bruce Waltke points out that "Wisdom of Solomon uses the Greek words *ho kosmos* to refer to Genesis 1:1." "Creation Account in Genesis 1:1–3," *BSac* 132, no. 527 (1975): 218.

4. I intend to show the progression of the chaos–cosmos theme in broad historical strokes as it develops in the canon as we have it: Genesis-Exodus-Joshua; Wisdom-Psalms-Prophets; and in the New Testament, Gospels-Acts-Epistles-Revelation.

sea above the firmament and coming down through the windows of heaven, while the world's seas and lakes were thought of as being connected with the subterranean part of the cosmic sea (cf. Gen. 7:11)."[5]

The chaos–cosmos theme in Scripture has many similarities with ancient Near Eastern myths. According to the ancient Babylonian creation epic *Enuma Elish*, the Babylonian head god, Marduk, created heaven and earth when Marduk battled the ocean goddess Tiamat:

> The Lord spread out his net, encircled her,
> The ill wind he had held behind him he released in her
>   face.
> Tiamat opened her mouth to swallow,
> He thrust in the ill wind so she could not close her lips.
> The raging winds bloated her belly,
> Her insides were stopped up, she gaped her mouth wide.
> He shot off the arrow, it broke open her belly,
> It cut to her innards, it pierced the heart.
> He subdued her and snuffed out her life,
> He flung down her carcass, he took his stand upon it. . . .
> He split her in two, like a fish for drying,
> Half of her he set up and made as a cover, heaven.
> He stretched out the hide and assigned watchmen,
> And ordered them not to let her waters escape.
> He crossed heaven and inspected (its) firmament. . . .
> Spreading [half of] her as a cover, he established the
>   netherworld. . . .
> Then the great gods convened.
> They made Marduk's destiny highest. . . .

---

5. Day, *God's Conflict with the Dragon and the Sea*, 4.

They established him forever for lordship of heaven and
  earth. . . .
His word shall be supreme above and below.[6]

When Babylonian literature was rediscovered in the late nine-
teenth century, many scholars assumed that Israel simply took
over the Babylonian creation myth. For example, the influential
Hermann Gunkel claimed that the *Enuma Elish* was simply transferred to Israel, where it lost many of its mythological and poly-
theistic elements until "in Genesis 1 it is, as far as was possible,
completely Judaized."[7] As Robin Routledge points out, however,
"While there may be enough points of similarity to suggest that
the writer of Genesis knew the Babylonian myth and used some
of its imagery, it is widely recognized that there is nothing to indicate dependence. The conflict motif [battle against chaos] and
ultimate exaltation of the creator god which is a central feature of
Enuma Elish is missing from Genesis 1."[8]

---

6. *Enuma Elish*, tablet 4, lines 95–104, 137–141; tablet 5, line 63; and tablet 6, lines 95–96, 100, 104, as translated by Benjamin R. Frost in William W. Hallo, ed., *The Context of Scripture* (New York: Brill, 1996), 1:390–402.

7. Gunkel writes, "We have established the following religio-historical sequence concerning the creation myth:

1. *Marduk* myth . . .	The Babylonian myth is transferred to Israel;
2. Poetic recension of the YHWH myth . . .	There it loses many of its mythological elements and nearly all of its polytheistic elements;
3. Genesis 1 . . .	In Genesis 1 it is, as far as was possible, completely Judaized."

Creation and Chaos in the Primeval Era and the Eschaton: A Religio-Historical Study of Genesis 1 and Revelation 12, trans. K. William Whitney Jr. (Grand Rapids, MI: Eerdmans, 2006), 82.

8. Routledge, "Did God Create Chaos?," 72. Routledge continues, "Whilst *tĕhôm* [Heb. "the deep"] cannot derive from Tiamat, there appears to be general agreement that it is from the same root, and so may have been included as an intentional allusion to the Babylonian myth; though, significantly, in the Genesis narrative *tĕhôm* is not given divine status nor even personified." (73). Tsumura writes, "The background of the Genesis creation story has nothing to do with the so-called *Chaoskampf* [chaos battle] myth of the Mesopotamian type, as preserved in the Babylonian 'creation' myth *Enuma Elish*. In Gen. 1, there is no hint of struggle or battle between God and this *tĕhôm*—water." *Creation and Destruction*, 143.

Contemporary scholars are more likely to look for the background of the chaos–cosmos theme in ancient Canaanite literature.[9] Here we also find a myth about a storm god doing battle with a sea god. The storm god (controlling lightning, rain, and fertility) was Baal, and the sea god (the god of chaos) was Yam. Part of the Baal myth reads as follows:

> The mace whirled in Baal's hand like an eagle,
> (grasped) in his fingers it crushed the pate of prince [Yam]. . . .
> Yam collapsed and fell down to the earth,
> his face quivered and his features crumpled up.
> Baal was drawing up Yam and scattering him. . . .
> "Verily Yam is dead, (and) [Baal] shall be king."[10]

Although this myth also speaks of a god, Baal, battling the sea god for control, the result is not the creation of heaven and earth, but Baal's kingship and his building a palace in the heavens with windows to water the earth.

Biblical authors did not write in a vacuum, of course. To be understood, they had to accommodate their imagery to the prevailing culture, whether Babylonian, Canaanite, or Egyptian. Therefore Genesis, as well as other Old Testament books, must be heard against the background of the stories of the ancient Near East. But just as sermon illustrations using Little Red Riding Hood do not thereby teach that this fairy tale is literally and historically true, so the biblical

---

9. "Since the discovery of the Ugaritic texts from 1929 onwards . . . it has become clear that the immediate background of the Old Testament allusions to the sea monster is not Babylonian but Canaanite. The Ugaritic texts contain not only an account of Baal's defeat of the rebellious sea-god Yam, as a result of which he was acclaimed king, but also allusions to a defeat of Leviathan." Day, *God's Conflict with the Dragon and the Sea*, 4. Watson writes, "As a result of the Ras Shamra discoveries in the 1930s, it is now also generally held that the more immediate background of the so-called 'chaos' imagery is Canaanite, rather than Babylonian." *Chaos Uncreated*, 12.

10. The myth of Baal, formerly called "Anat," *Baal* 3A, 23–32, trans. G. R. Driver, *Canaanite Myths and Legends*, Old Testament Studies 3 (Edinburgh: T.&T. Clark, 1956), 83.

authors' use of ancient Near Eastern stories does not mean that they taught that these ancient stories were literally and historically true.

For example, Hebrew poetry called for the use of much imagery. Where were the Hebrew poets to get their imagery? From the stories known in that culture, of course—the ancient myths. Elements of those myths served to embellish the point they tried to make in order to make it more vivid. Instead of looking for similarities between the biblical writings and the ancient myths (often undertaken in order to establish dependence), it is more important to note the differences.[11] These differences make us aware of Scripture's criticism of the pagan myths.

Nahum Sarna has set out the relationship between the biblical references to chaos and those of the myths:

> The references appear to be snippets of what was once an epic about the God of creation and mutinous forces of primeval chaos at the outset of the cosmogonic process. The rebels are variously termed Rahab, Leviathan, sea monster(s) / Dragon (Hebrew *tănnîn*, pl. *tănnînim*); Sea (Hebrew *yām*, pl. *yāmmîm*), River(s) (Hebrew *nāhār*, pl. *nĕhārîm*); and Elusive Serpent (Hebrew *nāhāš bārīah*). Isaiah [51:9–10] tells that in primeval times, God's arm hacked Rahab in pieces, pierced Tannin, and dried up Yam, the waters of the great deep (Hebrew *tĕhôm*). Habakkuk [3:8] refers to God's wrath at Neharim and His rage against Yam. The Psalms [74:13–14; see 77:17] depict God driving back Yam with His might, smashing the heads of the monsters on the waters, crushing the heads of Leviathan, crushing Rahab so that he was like a

---

11. Terrence Fretheim, *God and World in the Old Testament*, notes the following dissimilarities: "Emphasis upon history rather than nature, the lack of theogony [birth of gods] and a conflict among the gods, the absence of interest in primeval chaos, the prevailing monotheism, and the high value given human beings" (66).

corpse, and scattering His enemies with His powerful arm.
. . . Similar echoes of this myth are found in Job [7:12], who
asks God, 'Am I Yam or Tannin that You have set a watch over
me?' In another passage, Job [9:13] states that God does not
restrain His anger; beneath Him, Rahab's helpers fall pros-
trate. He stilled the sea, struck down Rahab, and pierced the
Elusive Serpent [26:12–13].[12]

Although the Bible uses the same names as the ancient myths,
Sarna continues, "What fundamentally distinguishes the biblical references from the other Near Eastern examples is the Israelite, thoroughly monotheistic atmosphere: there is one supreme sovereign
God; His foes are not divine beings; the motif of theogony, or birth
of gods, is wholly absent; there are no titanic battles in which the
outcome appears to be in doubt at one time or another; there is no
mention of creation as a consequence of victory in combat; and there
is an official, quite different, canonical Genesis creation narrative
which expresses numerous polemical, anti-mythic elements."[13]

Aside from the "thoroughly monotheistic atmosphere," there is
another fundamental difference between Israel's faith and that of its
neighbors. Bernard Anderson explains:

By and large the religions of Israel's neighbors were tied to
the sphere of *nature*, where the cyclical rhythms were deter-
minative for man's existence. Israel parted with the religions
of the ancient Near East by declaring that *history* is the area
of ultimate meaning precisely because God has chosen to
make himself known in historical events and to call men to
participate in his historical purpose. . . . Israel broke with pa-
ganism, and its mythical view of reality, at the crucial point:

---

12. Sarna, *On the Book of Psalms*, 57–58.
13. Sarna, *On the Book of Psalms*, 59.

nature is not the realm of the divine. The God Israel worships is the Lord of nature, but is not the soul of nature. Israel's sense of God's transcendence resulted in "the emancipation of thought from myth."[14]

---

14. Anderson, *Creation Versus Chaos*, 27, 32. Anderson also says, "In contrast to religions which depreciate history and consequently dehistoricize man, the Bible sets forth a historical drama—a *Heilsgeschichte*—in which man becomes 'truly himself' as a historical being who decides and acts in response to the action of God in history. . . . According to biblical faith, our historical existence is enfolded within the plan and purpose of the God who is not a phe-nomenon of history but the Lord of history, who is not a power immanent in nature but the sovereign Creator—the God whose purpose and presence were made known in Israel's historical experience and in the fullness of time, according to Christian faith, in Jesus Christ" (30, 41–42).

Questions for Reflection

1. The Bible writers seem to accept the ancient Near Eastern view of a three-storied universe. For example, one of the ten commandments stipulates, "You shall not make for yourself a carved image, or any likeness of anything that is *in heaven above*, or that is *in the earth beneath*, or that is *in the water under the earth*" (Ex. 20:4). Can you give some more biblical evidence that the Bible writers assumed a three-storied universe? Check, for instance, Genesis 1; Genesis 7–8; and Psalms 24 and 104.

2. Does it bother you that the Bible writers seems to accept a three-storied universe? Why or why not?

3. Give some reasons why the Bible writers would use this ancient worldview.

4. What is our definition of *chaos* and *cosmos*?

5. List some of the words the Old Testament uses for what we would call "chaos."

6. The Bible writers use the same chaos–cosmos terminology as is used in the ancient pagan myths. Give some examples of this.

7. Give some reasons why the Bible writers would use the same chaos–cosmos terminology.

8. Carefully read Genesis 1. In contrast to the pagan myths, which considered chaos evil, where does Genesis 1 say that chaos was good?

9. Think of at least three other ways in which chaos in Genesis 1 is different from that of the ancient pagan myths (for the answers, you will have to look at some footnotes).

10. "What fundamentally distinguishes the biblical references [to chaos] from the other Near Eastern examples"?

11. What is another fundamental difference between Israel's faith and that of its pagan neighbors?

Chaos–Cosmos in Genesis

The foundations of the chaos–cosmos theme are laid especially in the book dealing with the beginning, Genesis.

FROM CHAOS TO COSMOS (GENESIS 1–2)

According to the ancient Near Eastern myths, as we have seen, the Babylonian god Marduk and the Canaanite god Baal both battled for control with the god of the sea (chaos). By contrast, in Genesis 1 God does not struggle with the forces of chaos, nor is chaos considered a god. In fact, in Genesis the primordial waters are not even personi-fied.[15] According to Genesis 1 it was *God* who created these waters and then, by merely speaking, turned chaos into cosmos.

Genesis 1:1 says, "In the beginning, God created the heavens and the earth." The NRSV translates verses 1–2 as a temporal clause, "In the beginning when God created the heavens and the earth, the earth was a formless void and darkness covered the face of the deep. . . ." Bernard Anderson judges that although this translation is grammati-cally possible, "it poses exegetical difficulties. Chief of these is the problem that the Priestly writer [of Genesis], who intends to stress the transcendence of God as the sole source of all that is, would be adopting the ancient mythical view of a preexistent chaos, indepen-dent of God. It is therefore best to follow the Septuagint [the Greek translation of the Hebrew Old Testament] and to read Genesis 1:1 as a complete sentence, a reading which is as defensible grammatically as the translation which makes it part of a temporal clause."[16] Moreover,

---

15. Although "the beginning condition in Genesis consists of primordial cosmic waters as attested throughout the ancient world, this beginning state has no personality and offers no opposition." Walton, "Creation in Genesis 1:1–2:3 and the Ancient Near East," 57–58. Walton continues, "Even as it operates within the ancient cognitive environment by dealing with func-tions, it does so from its intentional monotheism in which there are no threats, no rebels, no conflict, and no need to overcome obstacles" (60).

16. Anderson, *Creation Versus Chaos*, 111. Hubbard writes, "Genesis 1:1 performs a double literary function in the narrative: it serves both as a title for 1:2–2:1 and as a summary claim that God created everything (the 'what'). This means . . . that what follows (1:2–2:1) fleshes out the

starting with a complete, independent sentence is in harmony with the generational structure of Genesis where an independent sentence, "These are the generations of . . ." introduces a new sequence a full ten times: Genesis 2:4; 5:1; 6:9; 10:1; 11:10, 27; 25:12, 19; 36:1; and 37:2.[17] Along with the ESV and the NIV, therefore, we will understand verse 1 as a complete sentence, which breaks with the ancient chaos myth of a preexistent chaos by declaring, "In the beginning, God created the heavens and the earth."[18] God is the Creator of everything in the universe ("*the heavens and the earth*" and everything in between).[19] In other words, verse 1 speaks of the result of God's creative activity over seven days, which was an orderly universe.[20] As Robert Hubbard puts it, "Verse 1 narrates that God created the universe (earth included), while verse 2 describes earth's conditions immediately after its creation."[21]

---

details of that claim (the 'how')." "The Spirit and Creation," 72. See also Brevard Childs, *Myth and Reality in the Old Testament*, 39–40; Bruce Waltke, "Creation Account in Genesis 1:1–3," *BSac* 132 #527 (1975): 224; John Walton, *Genesis 1 as Ancient Cosmology*, 123–27; and Richard Davidson, "The Genesis Account of Origins," 61–69. For various positions on this issue, see Routledge, "Did God Create Chaos?," 75–81.

17. See my *Preaching Christ from Genesis*, 16. The NRSV wrongly concludes the foregoing section with the *tôlĕdôt* of 2:4a and begins the new section with verse 4b. It may do so to mark an inclusio between Genesis 1:1 and Genesis. 2:4a. But in doing so, it tears apart the AB/BA chiasm of 2:4, "These are the generations of *the heavens and the earth* when they were created, in the day that the LORD God made *the earth and the heavens*."

18. "The pregnant expression, 'in the beginning,' separates the conception of the world once and for all from the cyclical rhythm of pagan mythology and the speculation of ancient metaphysics. This world, its life and history, is not dependent upon nature's cyclical rhythm but is brought into existence as the act of creation by a transcendent God." Gerhard and Michael Hasel, "The Unique Cosmology of Genesis 1 against Ancient Near Eastern and Egyptian Parallels," 11.

19. This is the literary device known as *merism*, whereby two ends of a spectrum are understood to include everything in between.

20. Routledge observes, "One version of this [more traditional] view is that verse 1 describes the creation of this chaos. It seems more likely, though, that 'the heavens and the earth' as a compound expression refers (as in Gen. 2:1, 4) to the *ordered cosmos* rather than to a disordered preliminary stage in its creation. Genesis 1:1 would then be a summary statement which emphasizes (also taking account of the merism 'heaven and earth') that God is the sole creator of *everything*, and the detail of what that means is then set out in the rest of the chapter." Routledge, "Did God Create Chaos?," 77–78. See also Brevard Childs, *Myth and Reality in the Old Testament*, 30–42.

21. Hubbard, "The Spirit and Creation," 73. Hubbard's reasons: Verse 2 "opens with a noun ('Now the earth was . . .') rather than a verb—in other words, with a *disjunctive* clause. A *conjunctive* clause (a verb followed by a noun) would signal that verse 2 reports the next event after the event in verse 1. But the disjunctive clause of verse 2, as it were, hits the 'pause' button, freezing the action so the reader may focus on a single aspect of the cosmos introduced in verse 1, 'the

This means that verse 2 backs up from the cosmos described in verse 1 to the opening stage in God's creative activity and introduces us to what many have called "chaos."

The earth was *without form and void* (*tōhû*[22] *wābōhû*),
and *darkness* (*hōšek*) was over the face of *the deep (těhôm).*[23]
And the Spirit of God was hovering over the face of *the waters (ha māyim).*

This verse describes total chaos, piling up five words that will be used in later Scriptures either individually or in combination to refer to some form of chaos: "without form," "void," "darkness," "the deep," and "the waters." Genesis 1 adds two more words that refer to chaos: "seas" (*yāmmîm*) in verse 10, and "great sea creatures/monsters" (*tănnînim*) in verse 21, for the perfect number of seven words at this stage.[24] A few more words and synonyms will be added later in Scripture to allude to conditions of chaos. Note that this original chaos was not evil. God created it. In fact God called the "seas" and even the "great sea monsters" "good" (Gen. 1:10, 21).

---

earth'" (72–73). Hubbard adds in note 6, "In such cases, Hebrew grammarians categorize the function of the disjunctive clause as 'circumstantial' (i.e. it introduces the readers to specific circumstances in play at the time)." Accordingly, V. P. Hamilton translates verse 2 as: "And the earth—it was. . . ." *Genesis 1–17*, NICOT (Grand Rapids, MI: Eerdmans, 1990), 103.

22. "*Tōhû* (without form) [twenty times in the Old Testament] is used elsewhere to mean, in physical terms, a trackless waste (e.g., Deut. 32:10; Job 6:18), emptiness (Job 26:7), chaos (Isa. 24:10; 34:11; 45:18); and metaphorically, what is baseless or futile (e.g., 1 Sam. 12:21; Isa. 29:21)." Derek Kidner, *Genesis*, 44. See Childs, *Myth and Reality in the Old Testament*, 32. Hubbard writes "I propose that *tōhû wābōhû* be rendered 'lifeless wasteland.' The earth is 'lifeless' (i.e. uninhabited) and 'unproductive' rather than 'disordered' or 'shapeless.'" "The Spirit and Creation," 76. See also David Tsumura, *Creation and Destruction*, 22–35; and Eric Vail, *Creation and Chaos Talk*, (126–32).

23. "*Těhôm* here is simply a key, ancient cosmological term based on a common Semitic root (*tiham* [*at*], 'sea'). Specifically, *těhôm* designates 'deep, deep waters'—the cosmic, watery abyss that also appears in Egyptian and Phoenician cosmologies. . . . A few other passages understand that *těhôm* comprises both the primeval ocean now above the vaulted sky and the ground water that supplies the earth's surface (e.g., Gen. 7:11; Pss. 78:15; 104:6–16)." Hubbard, "The Spirit and Creation," 77. Hubbard continues, "No biblical text . . . portrays the deep as a power independent of God or as a personified entity capable of creating things on its own" (78).

24. Seven words for *chaos* is probably no coincidence in a narrative that uses seven and its multiples many times: seven days, seven times "and it was so," seven times "God saw that it was good/very good," twenty-one times (3 x 7) "earth," and thirty-five times (5 x 7) "God."

The initial description, "without form and void," "has been widely taken to refer to a primordial chaos, which was then transformed by God. This, again, appears deliberately to recall ancient Near Eastern mythology; though the absence of a conflict motif in Genesis 1 suggests that, as with *těhôm* [the deep], chaos is passive rather than in active opposition to the Creator. . . . The narrator in Genesis 1 is setting out an authentic and distinctive creation theology, but in so doing is willing to use familiar mythological imagery to present important ideas that might not easily be expressed in other ways."[25]

Was chaos present from the start, preexistent and eternal like God—as the ancient pagan myths taught and materialistic evolutionism today believes? Or did God create chaos? The biblical answer is clear. Only God is eternal and sovereign: "In the beginning, God created the heavens and the earth."[26] Therefore it was God who created the chaotic waters.[27] Psalm 95:5 declares "The sea is his, for he made it."[28] God can later use these waters for good (making the earth fruitful; Gen. 2:6; Ps. 104:10, 13) as well as for ill (Genesis 6–7, sending the flood). God alone is sovereign. In Isaiah 45:7 the Lord declares, "I form light [cosmos] and create darkness [chaos]; I make

---

25. Routledge, "Did God Create Chaos?," 73. Hubbard writes, "The divine breath/wind/spirit/ and the waters are not *warring* antagonists. Genesis 1:2 makes no overt reference to any battle or conflict as do other ancient accounts. . . . Rather, the contrast is between the moving, active, powerful, protective and life-giving 'spirit of God' and the stationary, inactive, powerless, unproductive and inert deep waters. The latter symbolize great potential for life and productivity present in the raw materials of Genesis 1:2 rather than hostile opposition." "The Spirit and Creation," 88.

26. von Rad observes, "The theological thought of ch. 1 moves not so much between the poles of nothingness and creation as between the poles of chaos and cosmos. It would be false to say, however, that the idea of the *creatio ex nihilo* was not present at all (v. 1 stands with good reason before v. 2!)." *Genesis*, 51.

27. "To portray the ultimate boundary of human history, that is, the creation, the biblical tradition makes use of traditional motifs which once circulated in pagan contexts with a completely different meaning." Anderson, *Creation Versus Chaos*, 39. Anderson also adds, "It must be reiterated that biblical monotheism tolerates no thoroughgoing dualism which traces the origin of the historical conflict between God and evil back before man to creation, in which case evil would be coextensive with the divine" (167).

28. See also Ps. 146:6: The Lord "made heaven and earth, the sea, and all that is in them"; and Proverbs 8:28: The Lord "made firm the skies above, when he established the fountains of the deep."

well-being [cosmos] and create calamity [chaos]; I am the LORD, who does all these things."

According to Genesis 1:2, then, all that existed at this point was a formless, empty, deep ocean covered in darkness. Nothing could grow on this earth; it was lifeless. But there was a ray of hope: "The Spirit of God was hovering over the face of the waters" (Gen. 1:2). Although the word for *Spirit* can sometimes be translated as "wind,"[29] in this context of God *speaking* (a full ten times "God said"), "Spirit" or "breath" is more appropriate.[30] The Spirit of God was not part of the chaos; it was hovering over (*mĕraḥepet ʿal*) the waters as an eagle hovers [flutters] over (*yĕraḥēp ʿal*) its young encouraging them to fly (Deut. 32:11). "The phrase [Spirit of God] conjures up images of a powerful force sent by God to influence both humans and nature."[31] The breath of God was about to speak and bring forth order, cosmos.

Then God spoke and, step by step, word by word, turned chaos

---

29. "Basically, the word means 'breeze' or 'breath,' but in some contexts it denotes 'wind' or 'spirit.'" Hubbard, "The Spirit and Creation," 78, with a reference to S. Tengstrom, "*rûaḥ*," *TDOT*, 13, 365–96. Hubbard summarizes his charts on the Old Testament use of *rûaḥ ʾĕlōhîm/yahweh* (80–81) as follows: "The *rûaḥ ʾĕlōhîm/yahweh* asserts incredible influence on people and nature: it 'stirs,' 'drives,' 'lifts,' 'throws,' 'brings out,' 'sets down,' 'makes,' 'blows on' and 'gives rest.' Startling things begin to happen with humans and in nature" (82). See also Walton, *Genesis 1 as Ancient Cosmology*, 146–51.

30. Hubbard offers three reasons for connecting "the *rûaḥ ʾĕlōhîm* (Gen. 1:2) and the subsequent 'words' spoken by *ʾĕlōhîm* (Gen. 1:3–31). . . . First, the biblical association elsewhere of the presence of the spirit with divine speech at least raises that possibility. . . . It is striking, then, that as soon as the *rûaḥ* line concludes (v. 2), the very next words report, 'And God said. . . .' Second, the narrative's literary flow seems to presume that connection. . . . Genesis 1 reports the active, powerful presence of the *rûaḥ* (v. 2) but not its exit from the scene. . . . Once it debuts, the *rûaḥ* fully participates in creation, empowering, if not executing, the series of divine words. . . . Finally, the assumption of spirit participation compares to the understanding elsewhere in the Old Testament: 'By the word [*dābar*] of the Lord the heavens were made, their starry host by the breath (*rûaḥ*) of his mouth' (Ps. 33:6 TNIV; cf. Pss. 147:18; 148:8). The synonymous parallelism implies a close connection between 'word' and 'breath.'" "The Spirit and Creation," 86–87. See also Tsumura, *Creation and Destruction*, 75–76; and Scott A. Ellington, "The Face of God as His Creating Spirit: The Interplay of Yahweh's *Panim* and *Ruach* in Psalm 104:29–30," in *The Spirit Renews the Face of the Earth*, ed. Amos Yong (Eugene, OR: Pickwick, 2009), 3–16, esp. 5–8.

31. Hubbard, "The Spirit and Creation," 85. Hubbard continues, "Simply and subtly the *rûaḥ ʾĕlōhîm* symbolically asserts the presence of Almighty God amid the darkness and the waters. That very presence affirms that the wasteland still stands under the sovereign sway of Yahweh. . . . The phrase here also asserts the presence of divine power—'primal energy' sent by God and poised to transform the scene in some obvious way" (89).

into cosmos: "God *said*, 'Let there be light [cosmos]' and there was light. . . . And God *said*, 'Let there be an expanse in the midst of the waters, and let it separate the waters from the waters.' And God made the expanse and separated the waters that were under the expanse from the waters that were above the expanse. And it was so. . . . And God *said*, 'Let the waters under the heavens be gathered together into one place, and let the dry land appear.' And it was so" (Gen. 1:3, 6–7, 9).[32] "The imagery is of a powerful sovereign who utters a decree from the throne . . . and in the very utterance the thing is done."[33] With his word, which is law, the sovereign God controlled the waters by setting their limits.[34] God channeled the waters so that they could make the earth fruitful.[35] Genesis 1:10 states, "God called the dry land Earth, and the waters that were gathered together he called Seas. And God saw that it was *good*." The gathered waters were not evil as in the ancient myths but good. According to verse 21, "God created the great sea creatures [sea monsters/dragons] and every living creature that moves. . . . And God saw that it was *good*." "The word 'good' carries the sense of correspondence to the divine intention, including elements of beauty, purposefulness, and praise-worthiness."[36] Now life could spring up on the earth.

As a climactic creative act, God said, "Let us make man in our image, after our likeness. And let them have dominion . . ." (Gen. 1:26). Humankind was special, the crown of God's creation. "And

---

32. "For he spoke, and it came to be; he commanded, and it stood firm" (Ps. 33:9); "By faith we understand that the universe was created by the word of God, so that what is seen was not made out of things that are visible" (Heb. 11:3); See also Ps. 148:5.

33. Walter Brueggemann, *Theology of the Old Testament*, 146.

34. See Psalm 33:7: "He gathers the waters of the sea as a heap; he puts the deeps in storehouses," and Job 38:8, 10–11: "Who shut in the sea with doors . . . , and prescribed limits for it and set bars and doors, and said, 'Thus far shall you come, and no farther, and here shall your proud waves be stayed'?"

35. See Psalm 104:9–10, 13: "You set a boundary that they [the waters] may not pass, so that they might not again cover the earth. You make springs gush forth in the valleys; they flow between the hills. . . . From your lofty abode you water the mountains; the earth is satisfied with the fruit of your work."

36. Fretheim, *Creation Untamed*, 13.

God saw everything that he had made, and behold, it was *very good*" (Gen. 1:31).

The second creation account follows up the first by reiterating that the absence of water was *not* good: "When no bush of the field was yet in the land and no small plant of the field had yet sprung up—for the LORD God had not caused it to rain on the land, and there was no man to work the ground, . . . then the LORD God formed the man of dust from the ground and breathed into his nostrils the breath of life, and the man became a living creature" (Gen. 2:5, 7). "Breathed is warmly personal, with the face-to-face intimacy of a kiss and the significance that this was an act of giving as well as making: and self-giving at that."[37] God placed humankind in a fruitful garden near life-sustaining water: "A river flowed out of Eden to water the garden, and there it divided and became four rivers" (Gen. 2:10). From the original chaos, God had created a beautiful, fruitful Paradise—an orderly cosmos.

In the book of Revelation, John describes the new heaven and the new earth and begins with an arresting observation: "Then I saw a new heaven and a new earth, for the first heaven and the first earth had passed away, and the sea was no more" (Rev. 21:1). The very first description of the new heaven and earth is that "the *sea* was no more." The implication is that the sea had become a symbol of evil that did not fit into the perfect kingdom of God. One of the questions we will pursue later is when and where the sea, chaos, turned so evil that it no longer had a place in God's perfect kingdom.

FROM COSMOS TO CHAOS: STRUGGLING EAST OF EDEN (GENESIS 3)

Unfortunately, God's good creation did not remain "very good" for long. The crown of God's creation disobeyed God. God had allowed

---

37. Kidner, *Genesis*, 60. Compare John 20:22: "And when he [Jesus] had said this, he breathed on them and said to them, 'Receive the Holy Spirit.'"

them to "eat of every tree of the garden," but God had said, "Of the tree of the knowledge of good and evil you shall not eat, for in the day that you eat of it you shall surely die" (Gen. 2:16–17). Tempted by "the serpent" (later identified as "that ancient serpent, who is called the devil and Satan" [Rev. 12:9]), they did eat of the tree of the knowledge of good and evil.

The effects of the fall into sin were felt immediately in the loss of innocence and the breakdown of harmonious relationships. "Then the eyes of both were opened, and they knew that they were naked. . . . and the man and his wife hid themselves from the presence of the LORD God among the trees of the garden. But the LORD God called to the man and said to him, 'Where are you?' And he said, 'I heard the sound of you in the garden, and I was afraid, because I was naked, and I hid myself'" (Gen. 3:7–10).

The man was afraid of the God who had so lovingly created him, breathing "into his nostrils the breath of life." God asked, "Have you eaten of the tree of which I commanded you not to eat?" The man then had the nerve to blame both God and the woman. Adam said, "The woman whom *you* gave to be with me, she gave me fruit of the tree, and I ate." The Lord God then turned to the woman, "What is this that you have done?" And she blamed the serpent: "The serpent deceived me, and I ate" (Gen. 3:11–13). The harmony of Paradise was broken: fear of God, blaming God and the woman, and blaming the serpent. Chaos invaded God's good creation.

Then followed God's judgment: "The LORD God said to the serpent, 'Because you have done this, cursed are you above all livestock and above all beasts of the field'" (Gen. 3:14).[38] The fact that the serpent was cursed "*above all livestock* and *above all beasts of the field*" suggests that the animal world is also living under God's curse. The

---

38. This is the first time we read in the Bible about God's curse. God's curse is the opposite of God's blessing (Gen. 1:22, 28; 2:3).

lamb has good reason to fear the wolf. The calf has good reason to fear the lion. With the fall into sin, chaos also invaded the animal kingdom.

The Lord continued addressing the serpent: "I will put enmity between you and the woman, and between your offspring and her offspring; he shall bruise your head, and you shall bruise his heel" (Gen. 3:15). Enmity between Satan and his offspring and the woman and her offspring will lead to much hardship in human history: "You shall bruise his heel." But ultimate victory is held out for the offspring of the woman: "He shall bruise your *head*"—a fatal wound.

With the fall into sin, the chaos of pain and suffering entered the world. To the woman God said, "I will surely multiply your pain in childbearing; *in pain* you shall bring forth children" (Gen. 3:16). And to Adam he said, "Cursed is the ground because of you; *in pain* you shall eat of it all the days of your life; thorns and thistles it shall bring forth for you; and you shall eat the plants of the field. By the sweat of your face you shall eat bread, till you return to the ground, for out of it you were taken; for you are dust, and to dust you shall return" (3:17–19).

The fall into sin resulted in pain in childbearing, pain in providing food, coping with thorns and thistles on a ground cursed by God, eating bread by the sweat of your face, and finally succumbing to the last enemy, death.

Then God drove them out of Paradise; they were to live east of Eden (Gen. 3:24).[39] Life had turned into a painful existence in a hostile, cursed world. The blessed cosmos of Paradise had turned into chaos—not the original chaos of Genesis 1:2 but now an *evil* chaotic world: struggles between animals and animals (3:14, see Isa. 11:6),

---

39. "Paradise is irreparably lost; what is left for man is a life of trouble in the shadow of a crushing riddle, a life entangled in an unbounded and completely hopeless struggle with the power of evil and in the end unavoidably subject to the majesty of death." von Rad, *Genesis*, 102.

between animals and humans (3:15), between husband and wife (3:12, 16), between nature and humans (3:17–19), and between humans and God (3:8–10, 12, 22–24).

Today we see this evil chaos east of Eden in the human race in the enmity between people, races, religions, and nation-states: wars, slavery, religious persecution, racism. We see this chaos in the swollen bellies of malnourished children; in people dying from cancer, Ebola, and other diseases and disasters; in the thousands of refugees fleeing their home countries, hundreds of them drowning as they cross dangerous seas in flimsy boats. We see this chaos in the violence perpetrated by drug cartels, in the senseless murders in our inner cities, in the rape of women and children,[40] and in the spread of terror organizations whose goal is to destroy people, nations, and cultural treasures.

In the book of Revelation, John describes the new heaven and the new earth where there will be no more tears, "and death shall be no more, neither shall there be mourning, nor crying, nor pain anymore, for the former things have passed away" (Rev. 21:4). As we have seen, John begins this description of the new earth with a striking observation: "Then I saw a new heaven and a new earth, for the first heaven and the first earth had passed away, and *the sea* was no more" (Rev. 21:1). The implication is that Scripture views our struggles with pain, disease, disasters, and death in this fallen world as a form of chaos that will one day be replaced by a well-ordered cosmos. God will turn our present painful living east of Eden into a harmonious cosmos on the last day, when Christ returns to usher in the perfect kingdom of God.

But even in punishing our ancestors for their rebellion, God

---

40. "The U.N. reports that 200,000 Congolese women and children have been raped during Congo's long-simmering conflict." Aryn Baker, "The Secret War Crime," *Time*, April 18, 2016, 38, http://time.com/war-and-rape/.

showed compassion and grace. There was still some order in the midst of the chaos. God still enabled humans to gather food from the cursed ground and to have children. Unfortunately, these children also rebelled against God. In only the second generation Cain murdered his brother Abel, the voice of his "brother's blood . . . crying to" God from the ground (Gen. 4:10). In the seventh generation Lamech bragged to his wives, "I have killed a man for wounding me, a young man for striking me" (Gen. 4:23). The chaos of violence was spreading on earth. At last the Lord intervened.

The Flood: Chaos to Restore Cosmos (Genesis 6–7)

"The Lord saw that the wickedness of man was great in the earth, and that every intention of the thoughts of his heart was only evil continually. And the Lord regretted that he had made man on the earth, and it grieved him to his heart. So the Lord said, 'I will *blot out* man whom I have created from the face of the land, man and animals and creeping things and birds of the heavens, for I am sorry that I have made them'" (Gen. 6:5–7).[41] Human wickedness had spoiled God's good creation so thoroughly that God decided to allow a chaotic flood to clean up his creation, killing all but a remnant in the ark with the righteous Noah. The flood was neither a natural disaster nor an accident. According to the Genesis account it was a deliberate act of God to cleanse the earth of that which had turned intrinsically evil (Gen. 6:11–13). The sovereign God removed his restraining hand and allowed his corrupted cosmos to return to chaos.

God again shows himself to be sovereign over the waters, and uses these waters to destroy evil. "In the six hundredth year of Noah's life, in the second month, on the seventeenth day of the month, on that day all *the fountains of the great deep* burst forth, and *the*

---

41. "The language of blotting out (6:7) suggests a wiping clean of the slate of the world and beginning anew." Fretheim, *God and World*, 81.

windows of the heavens were opened. And rain fell upon the earth forty days and forty nights. . . . And *the waters* prevailed so mightily on the earth that all the high mountains under the whole heaven were covered. . . . And all flesh died that moved on the earth, birds, livestock, beasts, all swarming creatures that swarm on the earth, and all mankind. . . . They were *blotted out* from the earth. Only Noah was left, and those who were with him in the ark" (Gen. 7:11–23). With Noah and all creatures in the ark God would make a new start to restore an orderly cosmos.

A NEW START WITH NOAH AND THE CREATURES IN THE ARK (GENESIS 8–9)

The turning point of the flood narrative is Genesis 8:1: "God remembered Noah and all the beasts and all the livestock that were with him in the ark." "This centering text shows that the attention of the text finally focuses on salvation rather than judgment, on what God does to preserve creation beyond the disaster, climaxing in the story of the rainbow and God's unconditional promise."[42]

"And God made a wind[43] blow over the earth, and *the waters* subsided. The fountains of *the deep* and the windows of the heavens were closed, *the rain* from the heavens was restrained, and *the waters* receded from the earth continually. At the end of 150 days *the waters* had abated, and in the seventh month, on the seventeenth day of the month, the ark came to rest on the mountains of Ararat" (Gen. 8:1–4). By restraining the waters the sovereign God turns chaos into a mix of chaos and cosmos: "chaos" because Paradise is not restored and God acknowledges that "the intention of man's heart is evil from

---

42. Fretheim, *Creation Untamed*, 46. Tikva Frymer-Kensky writes, "The flood is not primarily an agency of punishment (although to be drowned is hardly a pleasant reward), but a means of getting rid of a thoroughly polluted world and starting again with a clean, well-washed one" (150).

43. *Rûaḥ*. See also Genesis 1:2 and Psalm 104:30: "When you send forth your Spirit [*rûaḥ*], they are created, and you renew the face of the ground."

his youth" (8:21), and "cosmos" because God retains elements of his original creation order.

By drawing parallels with the creation account of Genesis 1, the narrator emphasizes that God is re-creating the world, making a new start with all the creatures in the ark.[44] As God had originally separated light ("Day") and darkness ("Night"), the waters above ("Heaven") and the waters below ("Earth" and "Seas") (Gen. 1:3–10), before life could flourish, so here God promised to maintain the separations that provided for an orderly cosmos: "While the *earth* remains, seedtime and harvest, cold and heat, summer and winter, *day and night*, shall not cease" (8:22). And as God had originally blessed Adam and Eve in Genesis 1:28 ("God blessed them. And God said to them, 'Be fruitful and multiply and fill the earth'"), so here, "God blessed Noah and his sons and said to them, 'Be fruitful and multiply and fill the earth'" (9:1).[45] Noah is the new Adam; with him and the creatures in the ark God is making a new start.

Then God made a covenant with Noah and all creatures. God said:

> "I establish my covenant with you, that never again shall all flesh be cut off by the waters of the *flood*, and never again shall there be a *flood* to destroy the earth." And God said, "This is the sign of the covenant that I make between me and you and every living creature that is with you, for all future generations: I have set my bow in the cloud, and it shall be a sign of the covenant between me and the earth. When I bring clouds over the earth and the bow is seen in the clouds, I will

---

44. God reigns over the chaotic waters (Gen. 1:6–9), here by closing "the fountains of the deep and the windows of the heavens" (8:2; see 7:11). "Early Judaism also understood the new world resulting from the flood to be a new creation (1 En. 106:13; Philo, Mos. 2.64–65; see Jub. 5:120)." Beale, *A New Testament Biblical Theology*, 60, note e.

45. "Unlike Atrahasis [the Babylonian flood story], the flood story in Genesis is emphatically not about overpopulation [as reason for the flood]. On the contrary, God's first action after the flood was to command Noah and his sons to 'be fruitful and multiply and fill the earth.'" Frymer-Kensky, "The Atrahasis Epic," 150.

remember my covenant that is between me and you and every living creature of all flesh. And the *waters* shall never again become a *flood* to destroy all flesh." (Gen. 9:11–15)

"In spite of human sin and violence, God has committed himself to his world; the unconditional covenant of the rainbow, by which he binds only himself, is a sign of that."[46] The bow was a weapon of war. But the rainbow in the clouds is a sign of God's weapon at rest: God is no longer targeting the earth. Brueggemann observes, "The bow at rest thus forms a parallel to the sabbath in 2:1–4a [2:1–3] at the resolve of creation. The first creation . . . ends with the serene rest of God. The re-creation (8:20–9:17) ends with God resting his weapon. God's creation is for all time protected from God's impatience."[47]

BABEL: THE CHAOS OF LANGUAGES TO RESTORE COSMOS (GENESIS 11)

Humankind soon rebelled against God again. Originally, God had given them the mandate "be fruitful and multiply and *fill the earth* and subdue it" (Gen. 1:28). After the flood, God repeated this mandate to Noah and his family: "And God blessed Noah and his sons and said to them, 'Be fruitful and multiply and *fill the earth*'" (9:1). But people thought they knew a better way to survive in a hostile environment. They would seek their security not in God but in their own power and glorious city. They said, "Come, let us build ourselves a city and a tower with its top in the heavens,[48] and let us make a

---

46. David J. A. Clines, "The Theology of the Flood Narrative," *Faith and Thought* 100 (1972–73), 128–42, esp. 140. Brueggemann writes, "The flood has effected no change in humankind. But it has effected an irreversible change in God, who now will approach his creation with an unlimited patience and forbearance." *Genesis*, 81.

47. Brueggemann, *Genesis*, 84–85.

48. "Here the addition 'to the heavens' shows they are vying with God himself. The Lord, not humankind, dwells in the heavens (Gen. 19:24; 21:17; 22:11, 15; Deut. 26:15; Ps. 115:16)." Waltke, *Genesis*, 179. von Rad writes, "The saga views such a development of power as something against God, rebellion against the Most High, as Babylon in many passages of the Bible is mentioned as the embodiment of sinful arrogance." *Genesis*, 151.

name for ourselves, *lest we be dispersed* over the face of the whole earth" (11:4).

How would God respond to this new rebellion? God had promised never again to send a flood that would destroy all flesh (Gen. 9:15). Yet, for the sake of his creation, God could not let humankind get away with their plan of relying on their ingenuity and unity for survival. The Lord said, "Behold, they are one people, and they have all one language, and this is only the beginning of what they will do. And nothing that they propose to do will now be impossible for them.[49] Come, let us go down and there confuse their language, so that they may not understand one another's speech.[50] So the LORD dispersed them from there over the face of all the earth, and they left off building the city" (11:6–8). Wenham states that this is "the decisive divine intervention that reverses the tide of human history. It is comparable to 'And God remembered Noah' in 8:1. Like 8:1, v 5 occurs at the midpoint of a story and heralds the undoing of what has gone before: there the flood waters start to fall; here the building stops."[51] Genesis 11 continues: "Therefore its name was called Babel, because there the LORD confused the language of all the earth. And from there the LORD dispersed them over the face of all the earth" (v. 9).[52]

Thus God used the chaos of different languages to stop the human rebellion in its tracks. Now, with humanity dispersed over

49. Wenham points out that "the structure . . . and sentiments closely resemble 3:22, 'Since man has become like one of us, knowing good and evil, now lest they reach out . . . and live forever. . . .'" *Genesis 1–15*, 240.

50. "God resolves upon a punitive, but at the same time preventive, act, so that he will not have to punish man more severely as his degeneration surely progresses." von Rad, *Genesis*, 149. Freitheim observes, "God . . . promotes diversity at the expense of any kind of unity that seeks to preserve itself in isolation from the rest of creation and thereby places creation at risk." *God and World*, 89.

51. Wenham, *Genesis 1–15*, 236.

52. "The name 'Babel/Babylon' does not mean 'gate of the god,' as the Babylonians held, but 'confusion,' and it evokes the similar sounding words 'folly,' and 'flood.' Far from being the last word in human culture, it is the ultimate symbol of man's failure when he attempts to go it alone in defiance of his creator." Wenham, *Genesis 1–15*, 245.

all the earth, God could again make a new start with one obedient person and his family.

The Lord's New Start with Abram/Israel (Genesis 12–47)

To initiate this new start for an orderly cosmos, God selected Abram, who lived in Ur of Chaldea (Babylonia). "Now the Lord said to Abram, 'Go from your country and your kindred and your father's house to the land that I will show you. And I will make of you a great nation, and I will bless you and make your name great, so that you will be a blessing. I will bless those who bless you, and him who dishonors you I will curse, and *in you all the families of the earth shall be blessed*.' So Abram went, as the Lord had told him" (Gen. 12:1–4).

God told Abram to separate himself not only from his country and his kindred, his more distant relatives, but even from his father's house, his immediate family. Abram was to go to a land the Lord would show him. God wanted to separate Abram from the nations for the time being so that, eventually, "in you all the families of the earth [would] be blessed." And like Noah before him, Abram obeyed God without questioning.

Then the "Lord," Yahweh, made a covenant with Abram:

Behold, my covenant is with you, and you shall be the father of a multitude of nations. No longer shall your name be called Abram, but your name shall be Abraham, for I have made you the father of a multitude of nations. I will make you exceedingly fruitful, and I will make you into nations, and kings shall come from you. And I will establish my covenant between me and you and your offspring after you throughout their generations for an everlasting covenant, to be God to you and to your offspring after you." (Gen. 17:4–7)

Abraham and his family thrived in the Promised Land. God had provided another "Paradise" for them: "the Jordan Valley was well watered everywhere like the garden of the LORD" (Gen. 13:10). Here they could flourish in peace and safety. God established his covenant also with Abraham's son Isaac (26:4, 24) and his grandson Jacob (28:13–15; 35:11–12). But when Jacob and his family suffered through drought in the Promised Land, they decided to move to Egypt, where Joseph governed (41:41). Again the family prospered: "Israel settled in the land of Egypt, in the land of Goshen. And they gained possessions in it, and were fruitful and multiplied greatly" (47:27). But soon their harmonious cosmos would turn into chaos.

Questions for Reflection

1. What are the seven words for *chaos* in Genesis 1?

2. List the forms of chaos introduced in Genesis 3.

3. List some other forms of chaos we experience in this world.

4. Give the two main biblical reasons why we experience chaos in this world.

5. How have you experienced chaos in your life?

6. The church fathers called Genesis 3:15 *protevangelium*, the first gospel. Explain why. See 1 John 3:8.

7. Give (again) our definition of *cosmos*.

8. List some forms of orderly cosmos in this world.

9. How have you experienced cosmos/order in your life?

10. Name the reasons why there is still some cosmos in this fallen world.

11. List the new starts God made with humanity according to the book of Genesis.

12. What do these new starts tell us about God?

13. What do these new starts tell us about God's promised new creation? (See, e.g., Isa. 65:17–25.)

Chaos–Cosmos in Exodus and Joshua

At the end of Genesis, Israel was flourishing in Egypt. But in time "there arose a new king over Egypt, who did not know Joseph" (Ex. 1:8). This king oppressed God's people with forced labor (1:11). He enslaved them and would not let them go. Forced labor and slavery are political forms of chaos. Pharaoh even commanded all his people, "Every son that is born to the Hebrews you shall cast into the Nile" (1:22). Egypt used the waters of the Nile to kill God's people. "And the people of Israel groaned because of their slavery and cried out for help. Their cry for rescue from slavery [chaos] came up to God. And God heard their groaning, and God remembered his covenant with Abraham, with Isaac, and with Jacob" (2:23–24).

Later the "Lord," Yahweh, said to Moses, "I also established my covenant with them *to give them the land of Canaan*, the land in which they lived as sojourners. Moreover, I have heard the groaning of the people of Israel whom the Egyptians hold as slaves, and I have remembered my covenant" (Ex. 6:4–5). Through a reluctant Moses, God would lead his people out of slavery (chaos) back to the Promised Land (cosmos).

Aaron's Staff Swallows up Pharaoh's Staffs (Ex. 7:8–13)

Exodus 7:8–13 has a subtle prelude to the chaos–cosmos theme in Exodus. Moses objected to going to Pharaoh demanding Israel's release because he thought the Egyptians would not believe that the Lord had sent him. So the Lord gave him a miracle to perform before Pharaoh. The Lord told Moses to throw his staff on the ground. "So he threw it on the ground, and it became a serpent (*nāḥāš*)" (Ex. 4:3). But when Moses actually performed this miracle before Pharaoh, the narrator tells us that his staff did not become a serpent but a dragon (*tănnîn*—a reference to chaos). We read in Exodus 7:8–13: "Then the LORD said to Moses and Aaron, 'When Pharaoh says to you, "Prove yourselves by working a miracle," then you shall say to Aaron, 'Take your staff and cast it down before Pharaoh, that it may become a serpent (dragon, *tănnîn*)."' So Moses and Aaron went to Pharaoh and did just as the LORD commanded. Aaron cast down his staff before Pharaoh and his servants, and it became a serpent (dragon, *tănnîn*). Then Pharaoh summoned the wise men and the sorcerers, and they, the magicians of Egypt, also did the same by their secret arts. For each man cast down his staff, and they became serpents (dragons, *tănnînim*). But Aaron's staff swallowed up their staffs. Still Pharaoh's heart was hardened, and he would not listen to them, as the LORD had said." Pharaoh would not listen even when threatened to be swallowed up by chaos.

As one scholar explains, "Variously translated as 'serpent,' 'dragon,' and 'sea-monster,' and used in parallel with 'Rahab,' and 'the Deep,' *tănnîn* [dragon] is not a garden-variety snake. To the contrary, it evokes the threat of chaos."[53] The fact that Aaron's staff "swallowed up" Pharaoh's staffs should have been a sign to Pharaoh that in the cosmic battle between the God of Israel and Pharaoh, the god of Egypt, the God of Israel would be the victor.[54] But Pharaoh's heart was hardened and he would not let Israel go. It would take a full ten plagues of chaos to convince Pharaoh to let God's people go.[55] And even then he changed his mind when he heard

---

53. Arie Leder, "Hearing Exodus 7:8–13 to Preach the Gospel," 97.

54. "The swallowing of the magicians' staffs by Aaron's . . . is a sign of the fate of the Egyptians at the sea. The only other use of the verb, *bālaʿ*, 'swallow,' occurs in 15:12, where it refers to the swallowing of the Egyptians in the depths of the earth beneath the sea." Fretheim, *God and World*, 115.

55. The first plague turned the fresh water of the Nile into blood, killing the fish (Ex. 7:14–25); the second saw the Nile teem with frogs, which would cover the land and even crawl into Pharaoh's bed (8:1–15); and the ninth covered the land with darkness (10:21–23) as in the original chaos (Gen. 1:2). Beal writes, "The plagues on Egypt that begin the process of the exodus are designed to indicate a de-creation and situation of chaos from which Israel can emerge through the division of water and earth as a new humanity on the other side of the Red Sea." *A New Testament Biblical Theology*, 172.

that Israel apparently got lost and was trapped behind the sea (Ex. 14:2–3).

Pharaoh and his army pursued Israel and "overtook them encamped at the sea" (Ex. 14:9). The Israelites complained bitterly to the Lord and Moses: "It would have been better for us to serve the Egyptians than to die in the wilderness" (14:12). But Moses said to them, "The LORD will fight for you, and you have only to be silent" (4:14).

THE LORD SAVES ISRAEL FROM THE SEA (EXODUS 14–15)

Pharaoh's armies were behind and the sea in front. Would the waters defeat Israel on its march to the Promised Land? The Lord told Moses what to do.

> Moses stretched out his hand over the sea, and the LORD drove the sea back by a strong east wind[56] all night and made the sea dry land, and the waters were divided. And the people of Israel went into the midst of the sea on dry ground, the waters being a wall to them on their right hand and on their left. The Egyptians pursued and went in after them into the midst of the sea, all Pharaoh's horses, his chariots, and his horsemen. . . .
>
> Then the LORD said to Moses, "Stretch out your hand over the sea, that the water may come back upon the Egyptians, upon their chariots, and upon their horsemen." So Moses stretched out his hand over the sea, and the sea returned to its normal course when the morning appeared. And as the Egyptians fled into it, the LORD threw the Egyptians into the midst of the sea. The waters returned and covered the

---

56. *Rûaḥ*. Compare Genesis 8:1: "God made a wind (*rûaḥ*) blow over the earth, and the waters subsided."

chariots and the horsemen; of all the host of Pharaoh that had followed them into the sea, not one of them remained. (Ex. 14:21–23, 26–28)

As with the flood, the Lord used the chaotic waters to save his people and to destroy those who defied him.

The Egyptians had enslaved God's people and attempted to destroy them by drowning their baby boys in the river Nile. Now God used the chaotic waters of the sea to eliminate the Egyptians instead. "But the people of Israel walked on dry ground through the sea, the waters being a wall to them on their right hand and on their left" (Ex. 14:29). Saved from the sea! As the Lord later promised through Isaiah, "When you pass through the waters, I will be with you" (Isa. 43:2).

Then Moses and the people of Israel sang this song to the Lord, saying,

I will sing to the Lord, for he has triumphed gloriously;
the horse and his rider he has thrown into the *sea*.
The Lord is my strength and my song,
and he has become my salvation. . . .
Pharaoh's chariots and his host he cast into the *sea*,
and his chosen officers were sunk in the Red *Sea*.
The *floods* covered them;
they went down into the *depths* like a stone. . . . [57]
At the blast of your nostrils the *waters* piled up;
the *floods* stood up in a heap;
the *deeps* congealed in the heart of the *sea*. . . .

---

57. "Throughout the text it is unmistakably clear that the waters and the primordial deeps are at the mercy of Yahweh's authority. [Exodus 15:5], for instance, specifically references the primordial deeps which Yahweh turns loose for his purpose, to cover Pharaoh's chariots and army. Later, in v 8, the waters stand up (at attention) like a wall at the 'blast of your [Yahweh's] nostrils.'" Mellish, "Creation as Social and Political Order," 169.

> You blew with your wind; the *sea* covered them;
>> they sank like lead in the mighty *waters*. . . .[58]
> The LORD will reign forever and ever. (Ex. 15:1–18)[59]

The sovereign Lord used the deadly waters to save his people Israel from the chaos of slavery in Egypt and to defeat their enemy. The cosmos of the Promised Land lay before them.

THE LORD DRIES UP THE JORDAN FOR ISRAEL (JOSHUA 3)

One more water obstacle remained before Israel could enter the Promised Land: the Jordan had flooded its banks and Israel could not pass over.

At the Lord's instruction, Joshua told Israel,

> "Behold, the ark of the covenant of the Lord of all the earth is passing over before you into the Jordan. . . . And when the soles of the feet of the priests bearing the ark of the LORD, the Lord of all the earth, shall rest in the waters of the Jordan, the waters of the Jordan shall be cut off from flowing, and the waters coming down from above shall stand in one heap." . . .
>
> As soon as those bearing the ark had come as far as the Jordan, and the feet of the priests bearing the ark were dipped in the brink of the water (now the Jordan overflows all its banks throughout the time of harvest), the waters coming down from above stood and rose up in a heap very far away,

---

58. "The poetry here moves well beyond the specific enactment of the Exodus and appeals to the language of the creator's victory over and administration of chaos." Brueggemann, "The Book of Exodus," 800.

59. "The 'Song of the Sea' (Ex. 15:1–18) praises Yahweh's victory in language which at times sounds like the myth of the battle with the waters of chaos. But it is quite clear that in this old hymn the enemy is Pharaoh's host, not the 'deeps' (*těhômôt*, vv. 5, 8), 'sea' (vv. 8, 10), or 'mighty waters' (v. 10)." Anderson, *Creation Versus Chaos*, 50. Day writes, "There is here no divine conflict with the waters, nor do the waters symbolize a foreign nation or nations; rather, Yahweh's victory at Yam Suph is over Pharaoh and his armies, and the waters, which are in no way personified, are merely the passive instrument used by Yahweh in accomplishing his purpose." *God's Conflict*, 98.

at Adam, the city that is beside Zarethan, and those flowing down toward the Sea of the Arabah, the Salt Sea, were completely cut off. And the people passed over opposite Jericho. Now the priests bearing the ark of the covenant of the LORD stood firmly on dry ground in the midst of the Jordan, and all Israel was passing over on dry ground until all the nation finished passing over the Jordan. (Josh. 3:11–17)

"The Lord of all the earth" controlled the waters of the Jordan, probably by causing a rockslide at Adam, where the Jordan passes through a narrow gorge. This would have caused the waters to rise "up in a heap very far away, at Adam," while the waters downstream would continue their way to the Dead Sea, leaving a dry river bed for Israel to cross over. "As recently as 1927 a blockage of the water in this area was recorded that lasted over 20 hours."[60] As God, at the Red Sea, could use "a strong east wind all night and made the sea dry land" (Ex. 14:21), so the Lord of all the earth could use a rockslide to control the waters. In any event, the Lord controlled the chaotic waters and brought his people safely into the Promised Land, another Paradise: "The Jordan Valley was well watered everywhere like the garden of the LORD" (Gen. 13:10).

————

Summarizing the chaos–cosmos theme we have covered thus far, we have seen pure chaos, pure cosmos, and a mix of the two. At its original level, chaos refers to the primeval chaotic waters that kept life from taking a foothold on earth. Although this was 100 percent chaos without any cosmos, it was *not evil* as in the pagan myths. It

---

60. *NIV Study Bible*, n. Joshua 3:13. This note also observes the connection between the Red Sea crossing and the Jordan crossing: "The Hebrew for 'heap' is found here, [v. 13 as well as] in v 16 and also in the poetic accounts of the 'Red Sea' crossing (Ex. 15:8; Ps. 78:13)."

was God who had created these waters and God who subsequently turned this chaos into cosmos through his creative words. But God did not eliminate the waters entirely; rather, he tamed them by confining them to the "Seas" which he called "good" (Gen. 1:10). Next God placed Adam and Eve in a fruitful garden watered by quiet rivers. The garden of Eden, Paradise, was truly a harmonious, 100 percent orderly cosmos.

When Adam and Eve disobeyed God's command, however, God banished them from Paradise. Living east of Eden, as we do today, involves chaos, disorder. This chaos is *evil* in that, as a result of sin, it involves pain, suffering, and death. But because of God's grace and faithfulness to his creation, there is still some order east of Eden: the succession of seasons and of day and night; the earth bringing forth vegetation; creatures thriving in the waters, the sky, and the earth; and human beings bearing children and finding food. Struggling for a living east of Eden is a mix of evil chaos and cosmos.

Subsequently, human sin ushered in other forms of evil chaos: Cain murdered his brother Abel; Lamech boasted of killing people for little or no reason (the chaos of anarchy). When the violence increased to the point of threatening God's orderly creation, God unleashed a worldwide flood. The chaotic waters cleansed the earth so that God could make a new start with those safe in the ark.

Later, at Babel, when people threatened God's design for his creation by disobeying God's mandate to fill the earth, God confused their language—another form of chaos. This confusion forced people to spread across the earth so that God could make a new start with Abram and his descendants, Israel.

Israel's enslavement in Egypt was another form of evil chaos. But God made a new start with Israel by controlling the wind and the Red Sea to send his people on their way to freedom in the Promised

Land.[61] When Israel approached the Promised Land, they could not enter because the waters of the Jordan were overflowing. Again God demonstrated his sovereignty over the turbulent waters by stopping the waters at Adam so that his people could pass safely on dry ground into the Promised Land.

Thus the overall message of the chaos–cosmos theme from Genesis to Joshua is that God is sovereign over both cosmos and chaos. He is able to turn chaos into cosmos, to control the chaotic waters, and to use the waters for good or ill as he makes new beginnings in seeking to fulfill his plan for a world that is truly a harmonious, orderly cosmos.

---

61. See Psalm 77:19–20: "Your way was through the sea, your path through the great waters; yet your footprints were unseen. You led your people like a flock by the hand of Moses and Aaron," and Isaiah 51:10: "Was it not you who dried up the sea, the waters of the great deep, who made the depths of the sea a way for the redeemed to pass over?"

Questions for Reflection

1. Exodus 7:8–13 tells the account of Aaron's "dragon" swallowing the Egyptian "dragons." What did this demonstration mean?

2. How is the account of Exodus 7:8–13 connected to the Egyptians later drowning in the Red Sea?

3. Name some similarities between the Lord saving Israel from the sea (Exodus 14) and the flood narrative (Genesis 6–7).

4. What do these narratives tell us about God and chaos?

5. Exodus 14:21 says that "the LORD drove the sea back by a strong east wind all night and made the sea dry land." Does the Lord's use of an east wind detract from the miracle? How is it still a miracle?

6. Can you think of other instances where the Lord used nature to perform his miracles? What does this say about the Lord?

7. How would you define a miracle?

8. At the drowning of the Egyptians, Moses, Israel, and Miriam sang, "I will sing to the LORD, for he has triumphed gloriously; the horse and his rider he has thrown into the sea" (Ex. 15:1, 21, the bookends of this song).[62] We still sing, "I will sing unto the LORD, for he has triumphed gloriously, horse and rider thrown into the sea." Do you think it appropriate to sing to the Lord when our enemies die? How would you justify this praise? Who gets the credit for Israel's salvation?

9. Would Jesus sing at the destruction of his enemies? (See Matt. 5:43–48; Luke 6:35; 23:34.)

10. How do you explain the different attitude toward enemies as you progress from the Old Testament to the New Testament? (But see already in the Old Testament Ex. 23:4–5; Lev. 19:18, and Job 31:29–30.)

---

62. In several Psalms Israel also celebrated this victory. See, for example, Pss. 74:13–14; 77:19–20; 78:13, 53; 106:9–12; and 114:1–5.

2

The Chaos–Cosmos Theme in
Wisdom, Psalms, and Prophets

The early chapters in Scripture lay the foundations of the chaos–cosmos theme. We have seen that, in contrast to the pagan myths, chaos was *not evil* but created by God as a first step in bringing about an orderly creation. God declared the gathered waters and even "the great sea creatures" (*tănnînim*, monsters) "good" (Gen. 1:10, 21). We have further seen that only in Genesis 1:2 was there 100 percent (good/not evil) chaos, and only in the pre-fall created order and Paradise was there 100 percent cosmos. But after the fall into sin, when God drove Adam and Eve out of Paradise, there was a mixture of evil chaos and cosmos: *evil* chaos because of human sin and God's curse, and cosmos because of God's faithfulness to his creation order. Even today we see evil chaos in this world as people struggle for a living on the cursed ground east of Eden, suffering from hunger, pain, disease, violence, and finally death. But we can also still count on some cosmos because of God's grace and faithfulness: the sun still "comes up" every morning, the seasons follow their God-ordained order, the earth brings forth food, and creatures still produce offspring.

In tracing the chaos–cosmos theme through the remainder of the Old Testament, we find the same emphases as in Genesis and Exodus, such as God being sovereign over chaos and the sea being good in some sense but evil in another. We find also greater specificity in personifying chaos and we meet two new characters associated with chaos: Leviathan and Rahab.

Chaos–Cosmos in Proverbs and Job

THE LORD CREATED BY WISDOM

The book of Proverbs touches on the chaos–cosmos theme only briefly in connection with the Lord creating the earth and the heavens by wisdom.

Proverbs 3:19–20 states:

> The LORD by *wisdom* founded the earth;
>> by understanding he established the heavens;
> by his knowledge the deeps (*tĕhômôt*) broke open
>> (*nibqāʿû*),[1]
>> and the clouds drop down the dew.

The hymn on wisdom in Proverbs 8 clarifies that the Lord brought forth wisdom before creating the chaotic waters and the earth:

> The LORD possessed me [wisdom] at the beginning of his
>> work,
>> the first of his acts of old.
> Ages ago I [wisdom] was set up,
>> at the first, *before the beginning of the earth.*

---

1. Compare Genesis 7:11: "All the fountains of the great deep (*tĕhôm*) burst forth (*nibqāʿû*), and the windows of the heavens were opened."

When there were no depths *(tĕhômôt)* I was brought forth,

    when there were no springs abounding with water *(māyim)*.

Before the mountains had been shaped,

    before the hills, I was brought forth,

before he had made the earth with its fields,

    or the first of the dust of the world.

When he established the heavens, I was there;

    when he drew a circle on the face of the deep *(tĕhôm)*,

when he made firm the skies above,

    when he established the fountains of the deep *(tĕhôm)*,

when he assigned to the sea *(yām)* its limit,

    so that the waters *(māyim)* might not transgress his

        command,[2]

when he marked out the foundations of the earth,

    then I was beside him, like a master workman,

and I was daily his delight,

    rejoicing before him always,

rejoicing in his inhabited world

    and delighting in the children of man. (Prov. 8:22–31)

As we see from the Hebrew words, Proverbs here deals with the same issues as does Genesis 1. In particular, verse 29 confirms that the Lord is sovereign over the chaotic waters. But Proverbs adds that even before God's creative activity described in Genesis 1, there was God's wisdom. In the New Testament, John will use this passage and Genesis 1 to witness to Jesus Christ: "In the beginning was the Word, and the Word was with God, and the Word was God" (John 1:1; see also Col. 1:17).

---

2. Compare Genesis 1:9: "And God said, 'Let the waters under the heavens be gathered together into one place, and let the dry land appear.' And it was so."

Job as Another Adam

The book of Job has much more to say about the chaos–cosmos theme. With allusions to Genesis 1–3, the narrator portrays Job as another Adam. As God breathed into Adam's "nostrils the breath of life, and the man became a living creature" (Gen. 2:7), so Job testifies, "The Spirit of God has made me, and the breath of the Almighty gives me life" (Job 33:4). The difference is that whereas Adam lived in the harmonious cosmos of Paradise, Job, reported to be "the greatest of all the people of the east (*qedem*)" (Job 1:3), lived "east (*miqqedem*) of Eden" (Gen. 3:24) where chaos disturbed cosmos.

The narrator begins: "There was a man in the land of Uz whose name was Job, and that man was blameless (*tām*) and upright, one who feared God and turned away from evil. There were born to him seven sons and three daughters" (Job 1:1–2). Job was not only blameless like Adam and Noah (*tāmîm*, Gen. 6:9) before him, but he also fulfilled God's mandate to "be fruitful and multiply" (Gen. 1:28; 9:1). *Seven* sons was a complete number of sons (compare to the seven days of creation) and a total of *ten* children was a full number of children (compare to the ten generations of Genesis).

But Satan, the personification of evil, that ancient serpent (Gen. 3:1), was also present to tempt Job to curse God. "The LORD said to Satan, 'Have you considered my servant Job, that there is none like him on the earth, a blameless and upright man, who fears God and turns away from evil?'[3] Then Satan answered the LORD and said, 'Does Job fear God for no reason?. . . . You have blessed the work of his hands, and his possessions have increased in the land. But stretch out your hand and touch all that he has, and he will curse you to your face.' And the LORD said to Satan, 'Behold, all that he

---

3. The Lord "holds up Job as one against whom 'the accuser' [*Satan* means "accuser"] can lodge no accusation." *NIV Study Bible*, Job 1:8n.

has is in your hand. Only against him do not stretch out your hand'" (Job 1:8–12).

As in Genesis 3, the Lord was sovereign over Satan but allowed Satan to tempt Job to disobey God. In one day Satan called up chaotic forces—enemies (Sabeans and Chaldeans) and forces of nature (lightning and a mighty wind)—to destroy all of Job's possessions: his oxen and donkeys, his sheep and servants, his camels, and finally his beloved children (Job 1:13–19). Yet Job did not curse God. Instead he "fell on the ground and worshiped. And he said, 'Naked I came from my mother's womb, and naked shall I return. The LORD gave, and the LORD has taken away; blessed be the name of the LORD.' In all this Job did not sin or charge God with wrong" (1:20–22).

Satan tried a second time to have Job curse God. Satan said to the Lord, "'All that a man has he will give for his life. But stretch out your hand and touch his bone and his flesh, and he will curse you to your face.' And the LORD said to Satan, 'Behold, he is in your hand; only spare his life.' So Satan went out from the presence of the LORD and struck Job with loathsome sores from the sole of his foot to the crown of his head. And he took a piece of broken pottery with which to scrape himself while he sat in the ashes. Then his wife said to him, 'Do you still hold fast your integrity? Curse God and die.' But he said to her . . . 'Shall we receive good from God, and shall we not receive evil?' In all this Job did not sin with his lips" (Job 2:4–10).

The closest Job came to cursing God was when he cursed "the day of his birth" (Job 3:1). In cursing his beginning, Job used the language of chaos, especially the "darkness" of Genesis 1:2. Job said:

> Let the day perish on which I was born,
>> and the night that said,
>> "A man is conceived."

> Let that day be *darkness*!
>> May God above not seek it,
>> nor light shine upon it.
> Let gloom and *deep darkness* claim it.
>> Let clouds dwell upon it;
>> let the *blackness* of the day terrify it.
> That night—let *thick darkness* seize it!
>> Let it not rejoice among the days of the year;
>> let it not come into the number of the months.
> Behold, let that *night* be barren;
>> let no joyful cry enter it.
> Let those curse it who *curse* the day,[4]
>> who are ready to rouse up *Leviathan*.[5] (Job 3:3–8)

Job wished to go back to the primeval darkness. He wished that he had never been born, that his day of birth would have been buried deep in the chaos of the original darkness, that his day of birth would have been swallowed up by chaos, namely by the sea monster Leviathan.

Leviathan

Leviathan is "the personification of the sea dragon."[6] In ancient pagan myths Leviathan was a sea monster that inhabited "the deep," the chaotic waters. It was "a repressive, anti-creation monster who swallow[ed] up life."[7] Job 41 provides an extensive description:

---

4. NRSV, "who curse the Sea." In arguing for the MT reading of *yôm* "day" rather than *yām* "sea," Day notes, "The cursing of the day no less than the rousing up of Leviathan is something generally considered undesirable, both bring darkness in their train." *God's Conflict*, 47.

5. "Using vivid, figurative language, Job wishes that 'those who curse days' [Eastern soothsayers] would arouse the sea monster Leviathan . . . to swallow the day-night of his birth." *NIV Study Bible*, Job 3:8n.

6. Tsumura, *Creation and Destruction*, 192. "The term 'Leviathan' is simply a poetic metaphor for huge sea creatures" (195).

7. Waltke, "The Creation Account in Genesis 1:1–3," 33.

Can you draw out *Leviathan* with a fishhook or press down his tongue with a cord?. . . . No one is so fierce that he dares to stir him up. . . . When he raises himself up the mighty are afraid; at the crashing they are beside themselves. He makes *the deep* boil like a pot; he makes *the sea* like a pot of ointment. [Synonymous parallelism equates "the deep" and "the sea."] Behind him he leaves a shining wake; one would think *the deep* to be white-haired. On earth there is not his like, a creature without fear. He sees everything that is high; he is *king over all the sons of pride.* (Job 41:1, 10, 25, 31–34)[8]

God Is Sovereign over the Sea, Leviathan, and Rahab

Like Genesis, Exodus, and Joshua, Job also stresses God's sovereignty over the chaotic waters. Job 38:8–11 speaks of God controlling the sea in the beginning:

> Who shut in the sea [*yām*] with doors
> when it burst out from the womb,
> when I made clouds its garment
> and thick *darkness* its swaddling band,
> and *prescribed limits* for it
> and set bars and doors,
> and said, *"Thus far shall you come, and no farther,*
> and *here shall your proud waves be stayed"*?

This sounds similar to Genesis 1:9: "And God said, 'Let the waters under the heavens be gathered together into one place, and let the dry land appear.' And it was so." But here "your *proud* waves" provides a hint of a conflict between God and the sea.

---

8. See Job 3:8 above and Isaiah 27:1: "In that day the LORD with his hard and great and strong sword will punish Leviathan the fleeing serpent, Leviathan the twisting serpent, and he will slay the dragon that is in the sea." Psalms 74:14 and 104:26 also mention Leviathan.

Job 26:7–13 makes the notion of conflict even more pronounced. The poem begins calmly enough, with God effortlessly stretching out "the north over the void," hanging "the earth on nothing":

> He stretches out the north over the void
>> and hangs the earth on nothing.
> He binds up the waters in his thick clouds,
>> and the cloud is not split open under them.
> He covers the face of the full moon
>> and spreads over it his cloud.
> He has inscribed a circle on the face of the waters
>> at the boundary between light and darkness. (26:7–10)

It sounds very much like God's effortless creative work in Genesis 1. But then the element of conflict, of battle, comes to the fore:

> The pillars of heaven tremble
>> and are astounded at his *rebuke*.
> *By his power he stilled the sea*;
>> by his understanding *he shattered Rahab*.[9]
> By his wind the heavens were made fair [the skies cleared];
>> his hand *pierced the fleeing serpent*. (26:11–13)

God had to "rebuke" the sea and still it with his power. He had to "shatter" Rahab—another personification of chaos. Job 9:13 expresses the battle even more strongly by referring to God's anger: "God will not turn back his *anger*; beneath him bowed the helpers of Rahab."[10]

---

9. Synonymous parallelism equates the sea and Rahab. "The name [Rahab] apparently means 'boisterous one,' an apt term for the personified raging sea. The fact that Rahab and 'the crooked serpent' *(nāhāš bāriah)* are mentioned in parallel verses in Job 26:12–13, and that Rahab is mentioned parallel to 'the dragon' *(tănnîn)* in Isa. 51:9, suggests that Rahab may simply be an alternative name for Leviathan, who is likewise called 'the crooked serpent' and 'the dragon' in Isa. 27:1." Day, *God's Conflict*, 6.

10. Compare Psalm 89:10: "You crushed Rahab like a carcass; you scattered your enemies with your mighty arm," and Isaiah 51:9: "Was it not you who cut Rahab in pieces, who pierced the dragon?"

So far we have seen that God is sovereign over chaos and controls the chaotic sea. In Job we have also seen the personification of chaos in the figures of Leviathan and Rahab. Here also the battle motif comes to the fore: chaos is not just passive but seeks to break out of the boundaries the Lord placed upon it, and in that sense is evil.

Questions for Reflection

1. What does the book of Proverbs contribute to the chaos–cosmos theme? Why is this important from a New Testament Christocentric perspective?

2. How does the narrator of the book of Job present Job as another Adam?

3. How does the narrator describe orderly cosmos in Job's life?

4. What is the meaning of the name *Satan*?

5. Why does God allow Satan to test the "blameless and upright" Job? Cite some biblical evidence to support your answer.

6. When did God allow Satan to test Jesus? How was God involved in this testing?

7. Does God also allow Satan to test us? (See Matt. 6:13; 1 Cor. 10:13; 1 Pet. 1:6–7; 5:8–11.)

8. How have you been tested by Satan?

9. What is Leviathan?

10. What is Rahab?

11. How does the narrator of Job present chaos as evil?

12. After utter chaos, how does God restore cosmos in Job's life? (See Job 42:10–17.)

13. No matter how much chaos your life is in today, what gives you hope for ultimate cosmos?

Chaos–Cosmos in Psalms

The psalms, being Hebrew poetry, use heightened imagery. The psalmists often got these vivid images from the stories that circulated in their culture. These images function as metaphors and therefore should be understood figuratively.[11]

The Lord Is Sovereign over the Sea and Made It Good

God's sovereign control of the sea by separating the waters (Gen. 1:6–10) is reflected in Psalm 33:7: "He gathers the waters of the sea (*yām*) as a heap; he puts the deeps (*těhômôt*) in storehouses."

Like Genesis 1:2, several psalms imply that the Lord made the sea good:

> The sea (*yām*) is his, for he made it,
>> and his hands formed the dry land. (Ps. 95:5)

> The earth is the LORD's and the fullness thereof,
>> the world and those who dwell therein,
> for he has founded it upon the seas (*yāmmîm*)
>> and established it upon the rivers. (Ps. 24:1–2)

The seas here are portrayed not as evil; in fact, they are *good* in that they support the earth.[12]

Psalm 104, a creation psalm, has the seas supporting not only the earth but even the Lord's "chambers" in heaven.[13] It also introduces

---

11. "The fragments of the Israelite conflict-myth appear exclusively in poetic texts, and in the Psalms and Prophets they are cited as literary devices to dress historical events in mythological terms for didactic purposes." Sarna, *On the Book of Psalms*, 59, illustrated by examples from Isaiah 30:7; Ezekiel 29:3; and Psalm 74:12–14.

12. See also Psalm 136:1, 6: "Give thanks to the LORD, for he is good. . . . to him who spread out the earth above the waters (*māyim*), for his steadfast love endures forever."

13. The seven strophes "parallel essentially the sequence of creative events in the Genesis story (vv. 1b–30)." Anderson, *From Creation to New Creation*, 86 (for details, see 217–19). See also Anderson, *Creation Versus Chaos*, 91–93, and Richard Davidson, "The Creation Theme in Psalm 104," 153–57.

a hint of conflict, with the Lord *rebuking* the waters and the waters taking to flight, but in the end it is the Lord who formed Leviathan, that ancient sea monster, to *play* in the sea:

> He [the LORD] lays the beams of his chambers on the waters
>> (*māyim*);
>> he makes the clouds his chariot. . . .
> You covered it [the earth] with the deep (*tĕhôm*) as with a
>> garment;
>> the waters (*māyim*) stood above the mountains.
> *At your rebuke they fled;*
>> *at the sound of your thunder they took to flight. . . .*
> You set a boundary that they may not pass,
>> so that they might not again cover the earth. . . .
> From your lofty abode you water the mountains;
>> the earth is satisfied with the fruit of your work. . . .
> Here is the sea (*yām*), great and wide,
>> which teems with creatures innumerable,
>> living things both small and great.
> There go the ships,
>> and *Leviathan*, which you formed to *play* in it.
>> (Ps. 104:3, 6–7, 9, 25–26)

Created and controlled by the sovereign God, the gathered waters were not evil, as the ancient myths proclaimed, but "good" (Gen. 1:10). Psalm 104:13 adds that the Lord uses the sea for good purposes by watering the earth.

Psalm 78, referring to Israel's exodus from Egypt, shows that the Lord can use the waters in several good ways:

> He divided the sea (*yām*) and let them pass through it,
>> and made the waters stand like a heap.

> In the daytime he led them with a cloud,
> > and all the night with a fiery light.
> He split rocks in the wilderness
> > and gave them drink abundantly as from the deep
> > > (*tĕhômôt*).
> He made streams come out of the rock
> > and caused waters (*māyim*) to flow down like rivers. . . .
> He led them in safety, so that they were not afraid,
> > but the sea (*yām*) overwhelmed their enemies.
> > > (Ps. 78:13–16, 53)

The Lord used the sea to save Israel from its enemies (v. 13), to provide Israel with water in the wilderness (vv. 15–16), and to drown Israel's enemies (v. 53).

Psalm 114 combines the Lord's making a path through the Red Sea as well as the Jordan.[14] Both are personified.

> When Israel went out from Egypt,
> > the house of Jacob from a people of strange language,
> Judah became his sanctuary,
> > Israel his dominion.
> The sea (*yām*) looked and fled;
> > *Jordan* turned back. . . .
> What ails you, O sea (*yām*), that you flee?
> > O *Jordan*, that you turn back? . . .
> Tremble, O earth, at the presence of the Lord,
> > at the presence of the God of Jacob,
> who turns the rock into a pool of water (*māyim*),[15]
> > the flint into a spring of water (*māyim*). (Ps. 114:1–3, 5, 7–8)

---

14. See also Psalm 66:6: "He turned the sea (*yām*) into dry land; they passed through the river (*nāhār*) on foot," and Isaiah 50:2: "Behold, by my rebuke I dry up the sea (*yām*), I make the rivers (*nĕhārôt*) a desert."

15. See Exodus 17:6 and Numbers 20:11.

Again, the Lord is sovereign over the waters, drying up the sea and the Jordan and providing his people with life-sustaining water.

The Sea and Its Creatures Are Urged to Praise the Lord

Psalm 148:4–8 urges the "waters above the heavens" and even the "great sea creatures and all deeps" to praise the Lord:

> Praise him, you highest heavens,
>> and you waters (*māyim*) above the heavens!
> Let them praise the name of the LORD!
>> For he commanded and they were created.
> And he established them forever and ever;
>> he gave a decree, and it shall not pass away.
> Praise the LORD from the earth,
>> you great sea creatures (*tănnînim*) and all deeps (*tĕhōmôt*),
> fire and hail, snow and mist,
>> stormy wind fulfilling his word!

Psalm 96 calls on the sea to roar with gladness:

> Let the heavens be glad, and let the earth rejoice;
>> let the sea (*yām*) roar, and all that fills it;
>> let the field exult, and everything in it! (Ps. 96:11–12)

Psalm 98 urges the sea and the rivers to join all the earth in making "a joyful noise to the LORD" (v. 4):

> Let the sea (*yām*) roar, and all that fills it;
>> the world and those who dwell in it!
> Let the rivers (*nĕhārôt*) clap their hands;
>> let the hills sing for joy together. (Ps. 98:7–8)

If the sea and its creatures are urged to praise the Lord, they cannot be inherently evil.

The Sea Can Be Evil

Some psalms indicate that the sea can challenge the Lord, and in that sense it is evil. For example, Psalm 93 repeats three times,

> The floods have lifted up, O LORD,
>> the floods have lifted up their voice;
>> the floods lift up their roaring.
> Mightier than the thunders of many waters (*māyim*),
>> mightier than the waves of the sea (*yām*),
>> the LORD on high is mighty! (Ps. 93:3–4)

Psalm 89 uses more vivid battle language in describing God's ordering of the primeval chaos.[16]

> You rule the raging of the sea (*yām*);
>> when its waves rise, you still them.
> You *crushed Rahab* like a carcass;
>> you scattered your enemies with your mighty arm.
>>> (Ps. 89:9–10)

Later Psalm 89 moves on to God's anointed servant, King David:

> The enemy shall not outwit him;
>> the wicked shall not humble him.
> I will *crush his foes* before him
>> and strike down those who hate him.
> My faithfulness and my steadfast love shall be with him,
>> and in my name shall his horn be exalted.
> I will set his hand on the sea (*yām*)
>> and his right hand on the rivers. (Ps. 89:22–25)

---

16. "This scene depicts Yahweh's triumphant battle with Yam and the monster Rahab, the primordial beasts. In the wake of Yahweh's battle with these enemies there emerges an orderly world that appears in a succession of cosmic pairs: heaven and earth, north and south, the mountains Tabor and Hermon, and finally the celestial throne (v. 15 [Eng. v. 14])." Mellish, "Creation as Social and Political Order," 173.

As the Lord crushed Rahab in the beginning, he will crush David's foes. David's rule over the sea and the rivers (the Mediterranean Sea and the Euphrates River) reflects God's rule over all things.[17]

The Lord Saved Israel from the Sea

Several psalms celebrate the Lord's saving Israel from the sea. These psalms use the names of gods in the pagan myths—the waters, the deep, and the sea—for the Red Sea. For example, Psalm 106 reads:

> He *rebuked* the Red Sea (*yām-sûp*), and it became dry,
> > and he led them through the deep (*tĕhōmôt*) as through
> > > a desert.
> So he saved them from the hand of the foe
> > and redeemed them from the power of the enemy.
> And the waters (*māyim*) covered their adversaries;
> > not one of them was left. (Ps. 106:9–11)

Psalm 77 is a lament in which the psalmist is in such deep trouble that he cannot sleep but recalls the Lord's "wonders of old" when the Lord delivered Israel from the sea:

> You hold my eyelids open;
> > I am so troubled that I cannot speak. . . .
> "Will the Lord spurn forever,
> > and never again be favorable? . . ."
> I will remember the deeds of the LORD;
> > yes, I will remember your *wonders of old*. . . .
> You are the God who works *wonders*;
> > you have made known your might among the peoples.

---

17. See John Stek, *NIV Study Bible*, Ps. 89:25n. Anderson writes, "Just as Yahweh, the Divine Warrior, is victorious over the powers of chaos, so the earthly king, the representative of the Deity, will be victorious over the mythical 'floods.'" *From Creation to New Creation*, 83.

You with your arm redeemed your people,
the children of Jacob and Joseph. *Selah*
When the waters (*māyim*) saw you, O God,
when the waters (*māyim*) saw you, they were afraid;
indeed, the deep (*těhōmôt*) trembled.
The clouds poured out water (*māyim*);
the skies gave forth thunder;
your arrows [lightning] flashed on every side.
The crash of your thunder was in the whirlwind;
your lightnings lighted up the world;
the earth trembled and shook.
Your way was through the sea (*yām*),
your path through the great waters (*māyim*);
yet your footprints were unseen.
You led your people like a flock
by the hand of Moses and Aaron.[18] (Ps. 77:4, 7, 11, 14–20)

Kevin Mellish writes, "The reference to these critical events of the past provided the writer with a sense of hope that God would help his people in the current threat they were facing."[19]

Psalms Call Israel's Enemies *Monsters* and *Leviathan*

Psalm 74 is another lament, probably bemoaning the destruction of Jerusalem in 586 BC. In recalling how the Lord saved Israel from slavery in Egypt, the psalm calls the Egyptians "sea monsters" and "Leviathan."

How long, O God, is the foe to scoff?
Is the enemy to revile your name forever? . . .

---

18. See also Isaiah 51:10: "Was it not you who dried up the sea, the waters of the great deep, who made the depths of the sea a way for the redeemed to pass over?"
19. Mellish, "Creation as Social and Political Order," 171.

Yet God my King is from of old,

    working salvation in the midst of the earth.

You divided the [Red] sea (*yām*) by your might;

    you broke the heads of the sea monsters (*tănnînim*)

        [Egypt] on the waters (*māyim*).[20]

You crushed the heads of *Leviathan*;[21]

    you gave him [Egypt] as food for the creatures of the

        wilderness.

You split open springs and brooks;

    you dried up ever-flowing streams.[22] (Ps. 74:10–15)

In calling enemies like Egypt and Babylonia "sea monsters" and "Leviathan," *chaos* takes on an even more personal connotation of evil.[23]

The Lord Can Save from the Chaos of Enemies and Death

Psalm 69 is a lament from a king who is surrounded by enemies seeking to kill him.

---

20. See also Ezekiel 29:3: "Behold, I am against you, Pharaoh king of Egypt, the great dragon (*tănnîn*) that lies in the midst of his streams, that says, 'My Nile is my own; I made it for myself,'" and Ezekiel 32:2–8. Isaiah writes: "Egypt's help is worthless and empty; therefore I have called her 'Rahab who sits still'" (30:7) and also: "Was it not you who cut Rahab in pieces, who pierced the dragon?" (51:9).

21. "The imagery is borrowed from ancient Near Eastern creation myths, in which the primeval chaotic waters were depicted as a many-headed monster that the creator-god overcame, after which he established the world order." Stek, *NIV Study Bible*, 74:13–14n. Day writes, "It has been established from the Ugaritic texts that Leviathan in fact possessed seven heads. . . . [Compare] "the seven heads of the 'dragon' in Rev. 12:3 and the seven heads of the 'beast' in Rev. 13:1 and 17:3." *God's Conflict*, 24.

22. The first part of verse 15 may refer to Exodus 17:6, where the Lord provided water for Israel from the rock, while the second part may refer to Exodus 14:29, where "the people of Israel walked on dry ground through the sea." But verse 15 may also be an allusion to the original chaos, "to springs cleft open so that the primaeval waters might be removed from the earth." Day, *God's Conflict*, 25. Anderson writes, "Here the mythopoeic language functions cosmologically, for the poet goes on to speak of the creation of springs and brooks, the alternation of day and night, and the establishment of the heavenly bodies, the fixing of the boundaries of the earth, and the creation of the seasons (vv. 15–17)." *From Creation to New Creation*, 84. Kraus observes, "Even though the mythical elements unquestionably predominate, undoubtedly also conceptions of ancient Israelite salvation history are present in vv 13ff. Both complexes have mutually impinged on each other." *Psalms 60–150*, 99.

23. "Various names for the dragon and the sea are applied to a nation or nations hostile to Israel. That this could be done is indicative of the fact that the powers of chaos, though subdued at the creation, were still liable to manifest themselves in the present on the historical plane." Day, *God's Conflict*, 88.

Save me, O God!

> For the waters (*māyim*) have come up to my neck.

I sink in deep mire,

> where there is no foothold;

I have come into deep waters (*māyim*),

> and the flood sweeps over me. . . .

Deliver me

> from sinking in the mire;

let me be delivered from my enemies

> and from the deep waters (*māyim*).

Let not the flood (*šibbōlet māyim*) sweep over me,

> or the deep swallow me up,

> or the pit close its mouth over me. . . .

Draw near to my soul, redeem me;

> ransom me because of my enemies! (Ps. 69:1–2, 14–15, 18)[24]

Psalm 46 states confidently that God is our refuge and strength and can deliver us from the rage of the nations:

God is our refuge and strength,

> a very present help in trouble.

Therefore we will not fear though the earth gives way,

> though the mountains be moved into the heart of the
> > sea (*yāmmîm*),

though its waters (*mêmāy*) roar and foam,

> though the mountains tremble at its swelling. *Selah.* . . .

The nations rage, the kingdoms totter;

> he utters his voice, the earth melts.

---

24. Psalm 144 also finds the king surrounded by enemies and begging the Lord to deliver him:

"Bow your heavens, O Lord, and come down! . . . Flash forth the lightning and scatter them; send out your arrows and rout them! Stretch out your hand from on high; rescue me and deliver me from the many waters (*māyim*), from the hand of foreigners" (vv. 5–7).

The LORD of hosts is with us;

the God of Jacob is our fortress. *Selah*. . . .

"Be still, and know that I am God.

I will be exalted among the nations,

I will be exalted in the earth!" (Ps. 46:1–3, 6–7, 10)

In Psalm 18 David teaches that God can even deliver one trapped in "the snares of death." David describes his troubles:

The cords of *death* encompassed me;

the torrents of *destruction* assailed me;

the cords of *Sheol* [the netherworld] entangled me;

the snares of *death* confronted me.

In my *distress* I called upon the LORD;

to my God I cried for help.

From his temple he heard my voice,

and my cry to him reached his ears. . . .

The LORD also thundered in the heavens,

and the Most High uttered his voice,

hailstones and coals of fire.

And he sent out his arrows and scattered them;

he flashed forth lightnings and routed them [David's

enemies].

Then the channels of the sea (*māyim*)[25] were seen,

and the foundations of the world were laid bare

at your *rebuke*, O LORD,

at the blast of the breath of your nostrils.

He sent from on high, he took me;

he drew me out of many waters (*māyim*).

He rescued me from my strong enemy

---

25. "Waters." The parallel passage, 2 Samuel 22:16, has *yām*, sea.

and from those who hated me,
　　for they were too mighty for me. (Ps. 18:4–6, 13–17)

The Lord, Enthroned over the Flood, Can Still a Storm

Psalm 29 hears "the voice of the LORD" (repeated seven times) in a thunderstorm that originated over the Mediterranean Sea and smashed into Lebanon, breaking its cedars. But the voice of the Lord "is *over* the waters," the Lord "sits enthroned *over* the flood."

The voice of the LORD is *over* the waters (*māyim*);
　　the God of glory thunders,
　　the LORD, *over* many waters (*māyim*[26]).
The voice of the LORD is powerful;
　　the voice of the LORD is full of majesty. . . .
The LORD sits *enthroned over the flood* (*mabbûl*[27]);
　　the LORD sits *enthroned as king* forever. (Ps. 29:3–4, 10)

In Psalm 107 the Lord stills a literal storm:

Some went down to the sea (*yām*) in ships,
　　doing business on the great waters (*māyim*);
they saw the deeds of the LORD,
　　his wondrous works in the deep.
For he commanded and raised the *stormy wind*,
　　which lifted up *the waves* of the sea.[28]
They mounted up to heaven; they went down to the depths
　　(*tĕhōmôt*);
　　their courage melted away in their evil plight;
they reeled and staggered like drunken men
　　and were at their wits' end.

---

26. "'The waters stand for tumultuous forces that threaten to overwhelm the regular order of life, in the way that a flood can overwhelm people, land, and even cities." John Goldingay, *Psalms* (Grand Rapids, MI: Baker, 2006), 1:417.

27. *Mabbûl* is used in Genesis 6–9 for Noah's flood.

28. In the Hebrew, verses 25 and 29 do not have "the sea" and verse 30 does not have "the waters."

Then they cried to the Lord in their *trouble*,
>and he delivered them from their *distress*.
He made the storm be still,
>and *the waves* of the sea were *hushed*.
Then they were glad that the waters were quiet,
>and he brought them to their desired haven. (Ps. 107:23–30)

The Lord Will Triumph over Rebellious Nations

Psalm 2 raises the issue of chaos in history when nations rebel against the Lord.

Why do the nations rage
>and the peoples plot in vain?
The kings of the earth set themselves,
>and the rulers take counsel together,
>*against the* Lord and against his Anointed, saying,
"Let us burst their bonds apart
>and cast away their cords from us." (Ps. 2:1–3)

Patrick Miller writes, "The fundamental and deepest question addressed by the psalm is whether the disorders of history are an indication that the forces of chaos still control, and whirl is king, or whether there is a power ruling in the cosmos that can bring order out of disorder and overcome the inevitably self-seeking and ultimately tyrannous character of all human powers."[29]

Psalm 2 answers confidently:

He who sits in the heavens laughs;
>the Lord holds them in derision.
Then he will speak to them in his *wrath*,
>and terrify them in his *fury*, saying,

---

29. Miller, *Interpreting the Psalms*, 88.

> "As for me, I have set my King
>   on Zion, my holy hill."
> I will tell of the decree:
> The LORD said to me [Israel's King], "You are my Son;
>   today I have begotten you.
> Ask of me, and I will make *the nations* your heritage,
>   and the ends of the earth your possession.
> You shall break them *with a rod of iron*
>   and dash them in pieces like a potter's vessel."
> Now therefore, O kings, be wise;
>   be warned, O rulers of the earth.
> Serve the LORD with fear,
>   and rejoice with trembling.
> Kiss the Son [submission to the Messiah],
>   lest he be *angry*, and you perish in the way,
>   for his *wrath* is quickly kindled.
> Blessed are all who take refuge in him. (Ps. 2:4–12)

Rebellious nations certainly promote much chaos in this world by disrupting God's good order for society. But in the end the Lord will gain worldwide victory through his anointed King. In Revelation 19, John alludes to Psalm 2: "Then I saw heaven opened, and behold, a white horse! The one sitting on it is called Faithful and True, and in righteousness he judges and makes war. . . . From his mouth comes a sharp sword with which to strike down *the nations*, and *he will rule*[30] *them with a rod of iron*. . . . On his robe and on his thigh he has a name written, 'King of kings and Lord of lords'" (Rev. 19:11, 15–16).

———

30. Instead of the Hebrew for "break," Revelation follows the Septuagint and translates, "rule." See also Revelation 2:27 and 12:5.

Wisdom Literature and Psalms not only confirm the chaos–cosmos theme of the earlier Bible books but add greater specificity with the personifications of chaos in Leviathan and Rahab, calling Israel's enemies "Leviathan" and "Rahab," focusing on death, Sheol, and the grave as forms of chaos, and holding out the hope that the sovereign Lord can triumph over chaos.

Questions for Reflection

1. Name some similar emphases regarding chaos–cosmos in Psalms as in the earlier books.

2. Name some additional forms of chaos identified in Psalms.

3. According to Psalms how does God use the sea for good?

4. According to Psalms how does God use the sea for ill?

5. Name some Psalms that consider chaos evil.

6. How do rebellious nations cause chaos today?

7. Do you think disease is a form of chaos? Explain.

8. Do you think death is a form of chaos? Explain.

9. When there were no more Davidic kings, the king of Psalm 2 (and other royal psalms[31]) came to be understood as the Messiah King who would establish God's righteous kingdom on earth. How do the royal psalms envision the coming kingdom?

10. Do you long for Jesus's second coming? Why or why not?

---

31. Psalms 18; 20; 21; 45; 72; 89; 101; 110; 132; 144:1–11.

Chaos–Cosmos in the Major Prophets

With many similar statements, the prophets build on the chaos–cosmos theme established in Genesis, Exodus, and Joshua and expanded in the Wisdom Literature and Psalms. The new dimension the prophets add is that they project God's control of chaos into the future toward a well-ordered cosmos, a new creation, paradise on earth. We shall start with the book of Isaiah, which has more references to chaos, creation, and new creation than any other prophet.

Chaos–Cosmos in Isaiah

Isaiah (740–700 BC) was a prophet in Judah when Israel was overrun by the Assyrians. The book of Isaiah covers a lengthy period of history: from the Assyrians taking Israel into exile (fall of Samaria, 722 BC), to the Babylonians taking Judah into exile (fall of Jerusalem, 586 BC), to the rise of Cyrus the Persian, who united the Medes and Persians to defeat Babylonia and allowed the Jews to return to Israel (538 BC).

Isaiah uses chaos imagery to picture the Babylonian exile in two ways. First, Judah was enslaved in a foreign land as their forebears had been in Egypt. Second, exile meant that the Promised Land was empty; it was in a state of chaos. Isaiah 6:11 exclaims:

Then I said, "How long, O Lord?" And he said:
"Until cities lie waste
    without inhabitant,
and houses without people,
    and the land is a desolate waste."

The Lord Is the Great Creator of All

Isaiah 45, like Genesis 1:2–5,[32] speaks of the Lord creating the original chaos of darkness:[33]

> I form light (*'ôr*) and create darkness (*hōšek*);
>> I make well-being and create calamity;[34]
>> I am the LORD, who does all these things. (Isa. 45:7)

Isaiah 45 continues to speak of the Lord creating the heavens and the earth:

> I made the earth
>> and created man on it;
> it was my hands that stretched out the heavens,
>> and I commanded all their host. . . .
> For thus says the LORD,
> who created the heavens
>> (he is God!),
> who formed the earth and made it
>> (he established it;
> he did not create it empty [*tōhû*],
>> he formed it to be inhabited!):
> "I am the LORD, and there is no other.
> I did not speak in secret,
>> in a land of darkness (*hōšek*);
> I did not say to the offspring of Jacob,
>> 'Seek me in vain (*tōhû*) ["in chaos," NRSV].

---

32. Five times light (*'ôr*), three times darkness (*hōšek*). See also the ninth plague, darkness (Ex. 10:21–23), which is referred to in Psalm 105:28: "He sent darkness, and made the land dark." See also Mark 15:33, which is almost identical to LXX Exodus 10:22: "And when the sixth hour had come, there was darkness over the whole land until the ninth hour."

33. Scholars are not agreed on this. See the informative article and references in Michael Deroche, "Isaiah 45:7 and the Creation of Chaos?," 11–21.

34. The two merisms indicate that the Lord made light and darkness, well-being and calamity, and everything in between. Amos also writes, "Does disaster come to a city, unless the LORD has done it?" (Amos 3:6).

I the LORD speak the truth;
> I declare what is right. (Isa. 45:12, 18–19)

Several times Isaiah portrays the Lord as the great Creator who, without effort, stretched out the heavens like a curtain. For example, Isaiah 40 says:

It is he who sits above the circle of the earth,
> and its inhabitants are like grasshoppers;
who *stretches out the heavens like a curtain*,[35]
> and spreads them like a tent to dwell in;
who brings princes to nothing,
> and makes the rulers of the earth as emptiness (*tōhû*). . . .
Lift up your eyes on high and see:
> who created these?
He who brings out their host by number,
> calling them all by name;
by the greatness of his might
> and because he is strong in power,
> not one is missing. . . .
Have you not known? Have you not heard?
The LORD is the everlasting God,
> the *Creator of the ends of the earth.* (Isa. 40:22–23, 26, 28)

Isaiah 51 speaks of the Lord not only stretching out the heavens but also stirring up the sea (chaos):

"I, I am he who comforts you;
> who are you that you are afraid of man who dies . . .
and have forgotten the LORD, your Maker,

---

35. Compare, "I am the LORD, who made all things, who alone stretched out the heavens, who spread out the earth by myself" (Isa. 44:24).

who *stretched out the heavens*
and laid the foundations of the earth, . . .
I am the LORD your God,
who *stirs up the sea (yām) so that its waves roar—*
the LORD of hosts is his name.
And I have put my words in your mouth
and covered you in the shadow of my hand,
establishing the heavens
and laying the foundations of the earth,
and saying to Zion, 'You are my people.'" (Isa. 51:12–13, 15–16)

God's Promise to "Never Again" Be Angry with His People

The Babylonian exile was for Judah like the flood, "the collapse of the known world."[36] In Isaiah 54 the Lord recalls his promise to "never again" send such a disastrous flood (Gen. 9:11):

"This is like the days of Noah to me:
as I swore that the waters of Noah
should no more go over the earth,
so I have sworn that I will not be angry with you,
and will not rebuke you.
For the mountains may depart
and the hills be removed,
but my steadfast love shall not depart from you,
and *my covenant of peace* shall not be removed,"
says the LORD, who has compassion on you. (Isa. 54:9–10)

God's Promise to Restore His People

Isaiah also refers to the Lord saving Israel from the sea, but now the sea is pictured as an evil enemy. In Isaiah 51 Israel cries out:

---

36. Day, *God's Conflict*, 91–92.

Awake, awake, put on strength,

    O arm of the LORD;

awake, as in days of old,

    the generations of long ago.

Was it not you who *cut Rahab in pieces*,

    who *pierced the dragon (tănnîn)*? [God's victory at

        creation]

Was it not you who dried up the sea (*yām*),

    the waters of the great deep (*tĕhôm*),

who made the depths of the sea (*yām*) a way

    for the redeemed to pass over? [God's victory at the Red

        Sea][37]

And the ransomed of the LORD shall return

    and come to Zion with singing;

everlasting joy shall be upon their heads;

    they shall obtain gladness and joy,

    and sorrow and sighing shall flee away. (Isa. 51:9–11)

In verse 9 we meet Rahab again, a personification of the primeval chaos. Rahab is the dragon (*tănnîn*; synonymous parallelism). Like Psalm 89, Isaiah portrays Rahab as an evil enemy, which the Lord had to cut in pieces. Then he moves on to God's victory over the sea and the great deep at the time of the exodus. "The prophet refers to the events of creation and the Exodus to remind the people that Israel will be a restored/recreated community and will return home to Zion with jubilation."[38] The Lord will turn chaos into another cosmos by returning Israel to the Promised Land. It will be a new exodus.

---

37. Compare Isaiah 63:13: "Who led them through the depths (*tĕhōmôt*)? Like a horse in the desert, they did not stumble."

38. Mellish, "Creation as Social and Political Order," 172. Cohn writes, "For Second Isaiah the way Yahweh had made a path through the sea for the fleeing Israelites was a further manifestation of his power over the forces of chaos—and that same power was now about to accomplish another saving miracle." *Cosmos, Chaos and the World to Come*, 153." See also Day, *God's Conflict*,

Isaiah Calls Israel's Enemies, *Waters*, *Rahab*, and *Leviathan*

As some psalms called Israel's enemies Rahab and Leviathan, so Isaiah likens Assyria to evil waters that flood the land. Isaiah 8:7–8 says, "Behold, the Lord is bringing up against them [Israel] the *waters* of the River [Euphrates], mighty and many, *the king of Assyria* and all his glory. And it will rise over all its channels and go over all its banks, and it will sweep on into Judah, it will overflow and pass on, reaching even to the neck, and its outspread wings will fill the breadth of your land, O Immanuel."

Isaiah also uses the name *Rahab* as a nickname for Egypt. When Israel seeks refuge from its enemies in Egypt, the Lord declares in Isaiah 30:

> "Ah, stubborn children . . . ,
> who set out to go down to Egypt,
>   without asking for my direction,
> to take refuge in the protection of Pharaoh
>   and to seek shelter in the shadow of Egypt! . . .
> Egypt's help is worthless and empty;
>   therefore I have called her
>   'Rahab who sits still.'" (Isa. 30:1–2, 7)

Isaiah 17 graphically describes the evil, chaotic nature of Israel's enemies, who will flee at the Lord's rebuke.

> Ah, the thunder of many peoples;
>   they thunder like the thundering of the sea (*yāmmîm*)!
> Ah, the roar of nations;
>   they roar like the roaring of mighty waters (*māyim*)!

91–92: "In this passage . . . we have a blending of God's victory over chaos at the creation, at the Exodus and in the coming deliverance from the Babylonian exile. Rahab is both the monster defeated at creation and Egypt at the time of the Exodus and also, by implication . . . the thought is extended to Babylon at the time of the prophet himself. The return from exile in Babylon is both a new creation and a new Exodus."

The nations roar like the roaring of many waters (*māyim*),
> but he [God] will *rebuke* them, and they will *flee far*
> *away*,
chased like chaff on the mountains before the wind
> and whirling dust before the storm. (Isa. 17:12–13)

Isaiah 27:1 announces that it is the Lord himself who will punish Israel's enemies, here called "Leviathan": "In that day ['the day of the Lord'] the LORD with his hard and great and strong sword will punish *Leviathan* the fleeing *serpent*, Leviathan the twisting *serpent*, and he will slay the dragon (*tănnîn*) that is in the sea (*yām*)." Leviathan here "represents the terrible force of evil in the world. The symbol of triumph in the Day of the Lord is the destruction of this monster."[39]

The Lord Will Return Israel to the Promised Land

With allusions to the Lord drying up the Red Sea and the River Jordan, in Isaiah 43 the Lord promises Israel a new exodus, this one from exile in Babylon:[40]

But now thus says the LORD,
he who created you, O Jacob,
> he who formed you, O Israel:
"Fear not, for I have redeemed you;
> I have called you by name, you are mine.
When you pass through the waters (*māyim*), I will be
> with you;
> and through the rivers, they shall not overwhelm you;

---

39. Wallace, "Leviathan and the Beast in Revelation," 65. Anderson writes, "Since the sea symbolizes chaotic, demonic powers that were subdued by the Creator but not finally vanquished, apocalyptic writers looked to the future when the history-long conflict would be brought to an end." *Creation Versus Chaos*, 134.

40. "Just as Yahweh was victorious at the Reed Sea, driving back and conquering the waters of chaos, so in the time of the New Exodus he will show his mighty arm against powers opposed to his purpose." Anderson, *Creation Versus Chaos*, 128–29.

when you walk through fire you shall not be burned,
> and the flame shall not consume you.

For I am the LORD your God,
> the Holy One of Israel, your Savior.

I give Egypt as your ransom,
> Cush and Seba in exchange for you. . . ."

Thus says the LORD,
> who makes a way in the sea (*yām*),
>> a path in the mighty waters (*māyim*) [the exodus from
>>> Egypt],

who brings forth chariot and horse,
> army and warrior;

they lie down, they cannot rise,
> they are extinguished, quenched like a wick:

"Remember not the former things,
> nor consider the things of old.

Behold, *I am doing a new thing*;
> now it springs forth, do you not perceive it?

I will make a way in the wilderness
> and rivers in *the desert*.

The wild beasts will honor me,
> the jackals and the ostriches,

for I give water (*māyim*) in the wilderness,
> rivers in *the desert*,

to *give drink to my chosen people*,
> the people whom I formed for myself

that they might declare my praise." (Isa. 43:1–3, 16–21)

The "waters" are evil because they could "overwhelm" God's people (v. 2) but can also be used for good to drown Israel's enemies (vv. 16–17) and to enable Israel to survive in the desert (v. 20).

In Isaiah 44 the Lord repeats his promise that Israel will return to the Promised Land:

> Thus says the LORD, your Redeemer,
>> who formed you from the womb:
> "I am the LORD, who *made all things*,
>> who alone *stretched out the heavens*,
>> who spread out the earth by myself . . . ,
> who confirms the word of his servant
>> and fulfills the counsel of his messengers,
> who says of Jerusalem, 'She shall be inhabited' [cosmos],
>> and of the cities of Judah, 'They shall be built,
>> and I will raise up their ruins';
> who says to the deep, 'Be dry;
>> I will dry up your rivers;
> who says of Cyrus, 'He is my shepherd,
>> and he shall fulfill all my purpose';
> saying of Jerusalem, 'She shall be built' [cosmos],
>> and of the temple, 'Your foundation shall be laid.'"
>> (Isa. 44:24, 26–28)

The Lord Will Restore Paradise on Earth

In promising to restore Paradise on earth, the Lord promises to turn the chaos we experience east of Eden into a harmonious cosmos. We shall look at four passages: Isaiah 11:1–9; 25:7–8; 51:3; and 65:17–25. Isaiah 11 begins with the righteous reign of a new Davidic king who will usher in a new Paradise:

> There shall come forth a shoot from the stump of Jesse,
>> and a branch from his roots shall bear fruit.
> And the Spirit of the LORD shall rest upon him,

the Spirit of wisdom and understanding,

the Spirit of counsel and might,

the Spirit of knowledge and the fear of the LORD.

And his delight shall be in the fear of the LORD.

He shall not judge by what his eyes see,

or decide disputes by what his ears hear,

but with *righteousness* he shall judge the poor,

and decide with *equity* for the meek of the earth;

and he shall strike the earth with *the rod of his mouth*,[41]

and with the breath of his lips [his word] he *shall kill the wicked.*

Righteousness shall be the belt of his waist,

and *faithfulness* the belt of his loins.

[This Davidic king will usher in a new Paradise:]

The *wolf* shall dwell with the *lamb*,

and the *leopard* shall lie down with the *young goat,*

and the *calf* and the *lion* and the *fattened calf* together;

and a *little child* shall lead them.

The cow and the bear shall graze;

their young shall lie down together;

and *the lion shall eat straw like the ox.*

[Instead of chaotic predatory behavior, there will be peace and harmony even in the animal world.]

The *nursing child* shall play over the hole of the *cobra*,

and the *weaned child* shall put his hand on the *adder's* den.

[A beautiful picture of the return of an orderly cosmos: God's

---

41. See Psalm 2:9. Compare Revelation 1:16 (regarding the risen, glorified Christ): "In his right hand he held seven stars, from his mouth came a sharp two-edged sword"; and Revelation 19:15 (regarding the rider on the white horse): "From his mouth comes a sharp sword with which to strike down the nations, and he will rule them with a rod of iron."

punishment of enmity between the seed of the serpent and the seed of the woman (Gen. 3:15) will be lifted.]

> They shall *not hurt or destroy*
>> in all my holy mountain;
> for the earth shall be full of the knowledge of the LORD
>> as the waters (*māyim*) cover the sea (*yām*). (Isa. 11:1–9)

The formerly evil "waters" and "sea" can now function as a simile for the earth being "full of the knowledge of the LORD."

In Isaiah 25:7–8 the Lord promises to swallow up the chaos of death forever—a reversal of God's punishment of death for the human fall into sin (Gen. 3:19).

> And he will *swallow up* on this mountain
>> the covering [funeral shroud] that is cast over all
>>> peoples,
>> the veil [worn at funerals] that is spread over all nations.
>> He *will swallow up death forever*;[42]
> and the Lord GOD will *wipe away tears* from all faces,
>> and the reproach of his people he will take away from all
>>> the earth,
> for the LORD has spoken.

Isaiah 51:3 assures Israel that the Lord will turn her chaotic waste places into an orderly cosmos, like the garden of Eden:

> For the LORD comforts Zion;
>> he comforts all her waste places
> and makes her wilderness like *Eden*,
>> her desert like *the garden of the LORD*;

---

42. Compare Isaiah 66:22: "For as the new heavens and the new earth that I make shall remain before me, says the LORD, *so shall your offspring and your name remain.*"

joy and gladness will be found in her,

thanksgiving and the voice of song.

Isaiah 65 echoes Isaiah 11 that the Lord will restore Paradise on earth.[43] It does so as the climax to the "new things" Isaiah mentioned in chapters 42, 43, and 48;[44] it will be *a new creation*:

"For behold, I create *new heavens*

and a new earth,

and the former things shall not be remembered

or come into mind.

[The chaos of pain, sorrow, and death living east of Eden will be forgotten.]

But be glad and rejoice forever

in that which I create;

for behold, I create Jerusalem to be a joy,

and her people to be a gladness.

I will rejoice in Jerusalem

and be glad in my people;

no more shall be heard in it the sound of *weeping*

and the cry of *distress* [signs of chaos]. . . .

They shall build houses and inhabit them;

they shall plant vineyards and eat their fruit.

[Signs of cosmos: a reversal of God's punishment in Gen. 3:17: "In pain you shall eat of it all the days of your life."]

They shall not build and another inhabit;

they shall not plant and another eat;

---

43. "That which is interesting about these two visions [Isa. 11:1–9 and 65:17–25] . . . is their lack of more specific historical hints or handles; they are archetypal and ahistorical in many ways and therefore have been especially reapplicable as messages of hope later in tradition." Niditch, *Chaos to Cosmos*, 80.

44. Isaiah 42:9: "Behold, the former things have come to pass, and *new things* I now declare; before they spring forth I tell you of them." Isaiah 43:19: "Behold, I am doing a *new thing*; now it springs forth, do you not perceive it?" Isaiah 48:6: "From this time forth I announce to you *new things*, hidden things that you have not known."

for like the days of a tree shall the days of my people be,

and my chosen shall *long enjoy the work of their hands.*

They shall not labor in vain

or bear children for calamity [chaos],

for they shall be the offspring of the blessed of the LORD,

and their descendants with them [cosmos].

Before they call I will answer;

while they are yet speaking I will hear.

[Complete restoration of communion between the Lord and his people.]

The wolf and the lamb shall graze together;

the lion shall eat straw like the ox [no more predators],

and dust shall be the serpent's food.

[Not even the serpent shall prey on people.]

They shall *not hurt or destroy*

in all my holy mountain,"

says the LORD. (Isa. 65:17–25)

The orderly, harmonious cosmos of Genesis 1 and 2 will be fully restored.

Questions for Reflection

1. Name two ways in which Isaiah uses chaos language to describe the Babylonian exile and its results in Palestine.

2. Where and how does Isaiah portray the sea as evil?

3. Why does Isaiah call Israel's enemies "Rahab" and "Leviathan"?

4. In which books did we meet these names earlier?

5. How does Isaiah (especially chaps. 43–44) reveal the theme "from chaos to cosmos"?

6. How does Isaiah (chap. 11) picture the new creation as pure cosmos?

7. According to Isaiah, how will the new creation be similar to the world we inhabit now?

8. How will the new creation be different from the world we live in now?

9. Read again Isaiah 11:1–9 and 65:17–25. Which of these two images most capture your heart and imagination?

10. Do you long for God's promised new creation? Explain why or why not.

CHAOS–COSMOS IN JEREMIAH AND EZEKIEL

Jeremiah (626–587 BC) lived through the build-up to the Babylonian exile and was taken to Egypt by a band fleeing Judah. Though not as extensively as Isaiah, Jeremiah also uses the chaos–cosmos theme in his prophecies.

The Lord Is the Great Creator

Like Isaiah, Jeremiah proclaimed that the Lord is the great Creator who effortlessly stretched out the heavens. Jeremiah 10 says concerning the Lord:

> It is he who *made the earth* by his power,
> > who established the world by his wisdom,
> > and by his understanding *stretched out the heavens.*[45]
> When he utters his voice, there is a tumult of waters
> > > (*māyim*) in the heavens,
> > and he makes the mist rise from the ends of the earth.
> He makes lightning for the rain,
> > and he brings forth the wind from his storehouses.
> > > (Jer. 10:12–13)

Like Genesis 1:9–10, Jeremiah 5:22 also says that the Lord set boundaries for the chaotic waters of the sea:

> Do you not fear me? declares the LORD.
> > Do you not tremble before me?
> I placed the sand as the boundary for the sea [*yām*],
> > a perpetual barrier that it cannot pass;
> though the waves toss, they cannot prevail;
> > though they roar, they cannot pass over it.[46]

---

45. See also Job 9:8; Psalm 104:2; Isaiah 40:22; 42:5; 44:24; 51:13, 16; Jeremiah 51:15.
46. See also Job 38:8–11; Psalm 104:6–9.

Jeremiah 31 speaks of the fixed order of sun, moon, and stars God created (see Gen. 1:14–19). As God after the flood promised to uphold his creation order (Gen. 8:22), so he will uphold his people.

> Thus says the LORD,
> who gives the sun for light by day
>> and the *fixed order* of the moon and the stars for light by
>> night,
> who stirs up the sea (*yām*) so that its waves roar—
>> the LORD of hosts is his name:
> "If this *fixed order* departs
>> from before me, declares the LORD,
> then shall the offspring of Israel cease
>> from being a nation before me forever." (Jer. 31:35–36)

Jeremiah Calls Babylon's Devastation of Judah *Tōhû Wābōhû*

Going far beyond Isaiah, Jeremiah 4 likens Babylon's devastation of Judah to the "without form and void" (*tōhû wābōhû*) nature of the primeval chaos (Gen. 1:2).

> A lion has gone up from his thicket,
>> a destroyer of nations has set out;
>> he has gone out from his place
> to make your land a waste [chaos];
>> your cities will be *ruins*
>> *without inhabitant* [chaos]. . . .
> I looked on the earth, and behold, it was without form and
>> void (*tōhû wābōhû*) [chaos];
>> and to the heavens, and they had no light [chaos].
> I looked on the mountains, and behold, they were quaking,
>> and all the hills moved to and fro.

> I looked, and behold, there was *no man*,
> and all the birds of the air had fled.
> I looked, and behold, the fruitful land was *a desert*,
> and all its cities were laid *in ruins* [chaos]
> before the LORD, before his fierce anger. (Jer. 4:7, 23–26)

Jerusalem destroyed, the temple burned, the people taken captive to far-off Babylon—Jeremiah can think of only one phrase to describe this awful situation: *tōhû wābōhû*. This is the only time this combination describing the primeval chaos of Genesis 1:2 is repeated in the Old Testament. As if to underscore the allusion to the original chaos, Jeremiah adds the parallel line in verse 23: I looked "to the heavens, and they had no light (*ʾôrām*)." Genesis 1:3–5 used the word *light* (*ʾôr*) five times. Now there is no light. Darkness has descended on the Promised Land. Chaos has replaced cosmos.[47]

Jeremiah Likens Babylon's King to a Monster

Jeremiah 51 speaks of Nebuchadnezzar as a "monster" whom the Lord will punish. The inhabitants of Zion say,

> "Nebuchadnezzar the king of Babylon has devoured me;
> he has crushed me;
> he has made me an empty vessel;
> he has swallowed me like a monster (*tănnîn*). . . ."
> Therefore thus says the LORD:
> "Behold, I will plead your cause
> and take vengeance for you.

---

47. "In a terrifying vision the prophet portrays the results of a devastating invasion from the North. His poetic eye sees, however, not just the coming of the Foe from the North, but the invasion of chaos itself, as though the earth were returned to its primeval condition of 'waste and void.'" Anderson, *Creation Versus Chaos*, 12. Scholars disagree on whether Jeremiah 4:23–26 is patterned on Genesis 1:1–2:4. Compare, for example, M. Fishbane, "Jeremiah IV 23–26 and Job III 3–13: A Recovered Use of the Creation Pattern," *VT* 21 (1971): 152; and Tsumura, *Creation and Destruction*, 28–32.

> I will dry up her sea (*yāmmā*)
>> and make her fountain dry." (Jer. 51:34, 36)

The Lord Will Turn Evil Babylon into Chaos

As God earlier used the flood to eliminate evil, so the Lord will use the chaotic "waters" of Medo-Persia to punish Babylon. In Jeremiah 51 the Lord says that he will utterly destroy Babylon for its evil actions so that it will be total chaos:

> Thus says the LORD:
> "Behold, I will stir up the spirit of a destroyer
>> against Babylon. . . .
> For Israel and Judah have not been forsaken
>> by their God, . . .
> but the land of the Chaldeans is *full of guilt*
>> against the Holy One of Israel. . . .

> "I will repay Babylon and all the inhabitants of Chaldea before your very eyes for *all the evil* that they have done in Zion, declares the LORD.

> "Behold, I am against you, O destroying mountain,
>>>> declares the LORD,
>> which destroys the whole earth;
> I will stretch out my hand against you,
>> and roll you down from the crags,
>> and make you *a burnt mountain*.
> No stone shall be taken from you for a corner
>> and no stone for a foundation,
> but you shall be *a perpetual waste* [chaos],[48]
>> declares the LORD. . . .

---

48. Compare Jeremiah 50:12–13: "Behold, she shall be the last of the nations, *a wilderness, a dry land, and a desert.* Because of the wrath of the LORD she shall *not be inhabited* but shall be *an utter desolation.*"

The land trembles and writhes in pain,
>   for the Lord's purposes against Babylon stand,
to make the land of Babylon a *desolation*,
>   *without inhabitant* [chaos]. . . .
"How Babylon is taken,
>   the praise of the whole earth seized!
How Babylon has become a
>   *horror* among the nations!
The sea (*yām*) [Medo-Persia] has come up on Babylon;
>   she is covered with its tumultuous waves.
Her cities have become a *horror*,
>   a land of drought and *a desert*,
a land in which *no one dwells*,
>   and through which no son of man passes. . . .
Though Babylon should mount up to heaven [like Babel,
>   Gen. 11:4],
>   and though she should fortify her strong height,
yet *destroyers* would come from me against her,
>   declares the Lord.
"A voice! A cry from Babylon!
>   The noise of great *destruction* from the land of the
>   Chaldeans!
For the Lord is laying Babylon *waste* [chaos]
>   and stilling her mighty voice.
Their [Medo-Persia's] waves roar like many waters
>   (*māyim*);
>   the noise of their voice is raised,
for a *destroyer* has come upon her,
>   upon Babylon;
her warriors are taken;
>   their bows are broken in pieces,

for the Lord is a God of recompense;
he will surely repay."
(Jer. 51: 1, 5, 24–26, 29, 41–43, 53–56)

———

In 597 BC Ezekiel and other Jews were taken into exile by Nebuchad-nezzar. Ezekiel ministered in exile in Babylon from 593–573 BC. While in Babylon "the word of the Lord came to Ezekiel the priest, the son of Buzi, in the land of the Chaldeans by the Chebar canal, and the hand of the Lord was upon him there" (Ezek. 1:3). Like Isaiah, Ezekiel prophesied not only of God's judgment but also of God's grace.

The Lord Will Turn Egypt into Chaos

Among other prophecies, the Lord gave Ezekiel oracles of destruction against seven enemies of Israel: Ammon, Moab, Edom, Philistia, Tyre, Sidon, and Egypt (Ezekiel 25–32). His prophecy against the seventh, Egypt, was the most extensive. This prophecy was directed against Pharaoh Hophra (589–570 BC) who competed with Babylon for the capture of Jerusalem.[49] This Pharaoh bragged that the Nile was his because he had created it; in other words, he claimed to be the Creator God.

Ezekiel 29–32 contains seven prophecies against Egypt. In the first and last of these prophecies Ezekiel calls Pharaoh "the great dragon." Ezekiel 29 says that God will destroy Pharaoh for his haughtiness:

Thus says the Lord God:

"Behold, I am against you,
Pharaoh king of Egypt,

---

49. See Jeremiah 37:5–10; 44:30.

the great dragon [*tannîm*] that lies
  in the midst of his streams,
that says, 'My Nile is my own;
  I made it for myself.'
I will put hooks in your jaws,
  and make the fish of your streams stick to your
    scales;
and I will draw you up out of the midst of your streams,
  with all the fish of your streams
  that stick to your scales.[50]
And I will cast you out into the *wilderness* [chaos],
  you and all the fish of your streams;
you shall fall on the open field,
  and not be brought together or gathered.
To the beasts of the earth and to the birds of the heavens
  I give you as food [chaos]." (Ezek. 29:3–5)

Ezekiel 32 follows up with a picture of the dark *day of the Lord* striking Egypt in judgment:

Son of man, raise a lamentation over Pharaoh king of Egypt
and say to him:

"You consider yourself a lion of the nations,
  but you are like a dragon (*tannîm*) in the seas
    (*yāmmîm*);
you burst forth in your rivers,
  trouble the waters (*māyim*) with your feet,
  and foul their rivers. . . .

---

50. Because of the scales, some scholars think that the *tannîm* here refers to a crocodile. For references, see Day, *God's Conflict*, 94, n. 29. But Day argues cogently that *tannîm* here is the same mythical creature that is elsewhere called Leviathan (94–95).

> When I *blot you out*, I will cover the heavens
>> and make their stars *dark*;
> I will cover the sun with a cloud,
>> and the moon shall not give its light.
> All the bright lights of heaven
>> will I make *dark* over you,
>> and put darkness (*hōšek*) on your land,
>>> declares the Lord GOD." (Ezek. 32:2, 7–8)

Egypt will slide into darkness, that is, chaos. But in contrast to the darkness of the Lord's judgment of Egypt, Ezekiel ends with messages of hope for captive Israel and the Promised Land—cosmos.

The Lord Will Make the Dry Bones Live

Ezekiel 37 presents the graphic image of a valley of dry bones. The dry bones represent God's people in exile in Babylon. As the Lord led him through the valley, Ezekiel observed that the bones "were very dry" (v. 2)—"long dead, far beyond the reach of resuscitation," total chaos.[51] The Lord asked him, "Son of man, can these bones live?" And Ezekiel answered, "O Lord GOD, you know" (v. 3). Then the Lord told him to prophesy over the bones: "Thus says the Lord GOD to these bones: Behold, I will cause breath to enter you, and you shall live" (v. 5).

Next the Lord explained the vision of the dry bones: "Son of man, these bones are the whole house of Israel. Behold, they say, 'Our bones are dried up, and our hope is lost; we are indeed cut off' [chaos]. Therefore prophesy, and say to them, Thus says the Lord GOD: Behold, I will open your graves and *raise you from your graves* [cosmos], O my people. And I will bring you into the *land of Israel*. And you shall know that I am the LORD, when I open your graves,

---

51. *NIV Study Bible*, Ezekiel 37:2n.

and raise you from your graves, O my people. And I will put *my Spirit within you*, and you shall *live*, and I will place you in *your own land*. Then you shall know that I am the LORD; I have spoken, and I will do it, declares the LORD" (Ezek. 37:11–14). The Lord will bring Israel from exile back into the Promised Land—cosmos restored.

The Lord Will Restore Paradise in the Promised Land

Ezekiel 47 prophesies that, like the rivers in Paradise (Gen. 2:10–14), healing waters will flow from God's temple.[52] This will result in an abundance of creatures and all kinds of trees bearing fresh fruit and leaves for healing.

Ezekiel reports:

> Then he ["a man whose appearance was like bronze" (40:3)] brought me back to the door of the temple, and behold, water (*māyim*) was issuing from below the threshold of the temple toward the east (for the temple faced east). The water (*māyim*) was flowing down from below the south end of the threshold of the temple, south of the altar. . . .
>
> And he said to me, "Son of man, have you seen this?"
>
> Then he led me back to the bank of the river. As I went back, I saw on the bank of the river very many trees on the one side and on the other. And he said to me, "This water (*māyim*) flows toward the eastern region and goes down into the Arabah [the Jordan Valley], and enters the sea (*yāmmāh*); when the water flows into the sea (*yāmmāh*), the water (*māyim*) will become fresh [literally "healed," NKJV]. And wherever

---

52. Compare Joel 3:18: "And in that day the mountains shall drip sweet wine, and the hills shall flow with milk, and all the streambeds of Judah shall flow with water; and a fountain shall come forth from the house of the LORD and water the Valley of Shittim," and Zechariah 14:8: "On that day living waters shall flow out from Jerusalem, half of them to the eastern sea and half of them to the western sea. It shall continue in summer as in winter."

the river goes, every living creature that swarms will live, and there will be very many fish. For this water (*māyim*) goes there, that the waters of the sea (*yām*) may become fresh; so everything will live where the river goes. . . . And on the banks, on both sides of the river, there will grow all kinds of trees for food. Their leaves will not wither, nor their fruit fail, but they will bear fresh fruit every month, because the water (*mêmāyw*) for them flows from the sanctuary. Their fruit will be for food, and their leaves for *healing*." (Ezek. 47:1, 6–9, 12)

The very element which Genesis 1 used to describe chaos, "water," here issues from the temple and leads to an abundance of life. Even the sea, another symbol for chaos, will be healed and thrive with many fish. Since "sea" here refers to the Dead Sea, this message is even more astonishing. Paradise will be restored in the Promised Land.

In the New Testament John will extend the restoration of cosmos to all nations: "Then the angel showed me the river of the water of life, bright as crystal, flowing from the throne of God and of the Lamb through the middle of the street of the city; also, on either side of the river, the tree of life with its twelve kinds of fruit, yielding its fruit each month. The leaves of the tree were for the healing of the *nations*" (Rev. 22:1–2).

Questions for Reflection

1. Jeremiah 4:23 describes Babylon's devastation of Judah as "without form and void" (*tōhû wābōhû*). Apart from Genesis 1:2, this is the only other place in the Bible where this combination appears. What does this tell us about Babylon's devastation of Judah?

2. List at least five other words Jeremiah 4 uses to describe the chaos caused by Babylon.

3. In Jeremiah 51 the Lord promises to punish Babylon for the evil they have done in Zion. To get a sense of the range of chaos, read Jeremiah 51:41–58 and list at least seven words or phrases that describe the resultant chaos in Babylon.

4. Jeremiah 51:34 likens King Nebuchadnezzar to "a monster." Where have we run into the word *monster* before? In using this word for Nebuchadnezzar, what is Jeremiah saying about him?

5. Ezekiel prophesies primarily against Egypt which, like Babylon, had also tried to capture Jerusalem. Ezekiel 29:3 calls Pharaoh king of Egypt, "the great dragon." Ezekiel 32:2 says of Pharaoh, "You are like a dragon in the seas." What is the significance of Ezekiel using these words for Pharaoh?

6. In Ezekiel 32 the Lord promises to blot out Egypt. List the different words Ezekiel 32:1–8 uses to describe the resultant chaos.

7. Ezekiel 37:1–14 describes the chaos of the valley of dry bones. What is the significance of the description that the bones "were very dry" (v. 2)? Who are the dry bones? How will the Lord turn this chaos into cosmos? Which verses in this passage remind you of Genesis 2:7?

8. When the Lord, in Ezekiel 37:12, promises to "open your graves and raise you from your graves," how do you know that this refers not to the resurrection from the dead but to the return of the exiles to Israel?

9. Ezekiel 47:1–12 describes the vision Ezekiel received of Paradise restored in the Promised Land. Which words in Ezekiel 47 remind you of the words in Genesis 2:8–14 describing the original Paradise? What are the major signs of this restoration to orderly cosmos in the Promised Land? How do you know that Ezekiel, in contrast to Revelation 22:2, limits this Paradise to the Promised Land?

10. In Revelation 22 John extends this restoration of cosmos to all nations. On what basis can John include all nations?

Chaos–Cosmos in the Minor Prophets

The Minor Prophets reinforce the messages of the foregoing Old Testament books but, because of the threats of Assyria, Babylon, and the Medo-Persian Empire, they focus more on their contemporary circumstances and the future. Since this overview will be clearer if we organize it not by prophet but by subject matter, we shall review in turn what the Minor Prophets say about the Lord as the great Creator; the day of the Lord; the Lord controlling the wind, sea, and a great fish; the Lord controlling the rivers and the sea; and the Lord rebuking Satan.

THE LORD IS THE GREAT CREATOR

Like the earlier books, Amos (c. 760 BC) describes the Lord as the great Creator. In Amos 5:8 he speaks of the Lord making the stars, turning night into day and day into night, and watering the earth with the sea:

> He who made the Pleiades and Orion,
>> and turns deep darkness into the morning
> and darkens the day into night,[53]
>> who calls for the waters (*mê*) of the sea (*yām*)
> and pours them out on the surface of the earth,
>> the LORD is his name.

Amos 9:5–6 speaks of the sovereignty of God over chaos:

> The Lord GOD of hosts,
>> he who touches the earth and it melts,
> and all who dwell in it mourn,
>> and all of it rises like the Nile,

---

53. See the "fixed order" of day and night in Jeremiah 31:35: "Thus says the LORD, who gives the sun for light by day and the fixed order of the moon and the stars for light by night, who stirs up the sea so that its waves roar."

and sinks again, like the Nile of Egypt;
>who builds his upper chambers in the heavens[54]
and founds his vault upon the earth;
>who calls for the waters (*mê*) of the sea (*yām*)
and pours them out upon the surface of the earth—
>the LORD is his name.

THE DAY OF THE LORD

Like Isaiah and Ezekiel, Amos and Joel (c. 810–750 BC) present the day of the Lord as a day of darkness, not only for Israel's enemies but also for Israel itself. Niditch writes, "The judgment time involves a shaking up of the order of the cosmos such that certain features of that orderliness dissolve, creating a new chaos. The most often repeated image is of the darkening of the sun, moon, and stars, of their ceasing to function in their normal time-demarcating way."[55]

Amos 5:20 says, "Is not the day of the LORD darkness (*hōšek*), and not light (*'ôr*), and gloom with no brightness in it [chaos]?" In chapter 6 Amos warns Israel:

>Woe to those who are at ease in Zion. . . .
>Therefore they shall now be the first of those who go
>>into *exile* [chaos]. . . .

The Lord GOD has sworn by himself, declares the LORD, the God of hosts:

>"I abhor the pride of Jacob
>>and hate his strongholds,
>>and I will deliver up the city and all that is in it." . . .

---

54. Compare Psalm 104:3: "He lays the beams of his chambers on the waters."
55. Niditch, *Chaos to Cosmos*, 73.

"For behold, I will raise up against you a nation,
O house of Israel," declares the LORD, the God of hosts;
"and they shall oppress you from Lebo-hamath
to the Brook of the Arabah." (Amos 6:1, 7–8, 14)

Amos 8:9 adds, "'And on that day,' declares the Lord GOD, 'I will make the sun go down at noon and darken (*haḥăšaktî*) the earth in broad daylight.'" God's orderly creation will become undone.

In Amos 9:2–4 the Lord declares that there is no place to escape the judgment:

If they dig into Sheol,
from there shall my hand take them;
if they climb up to heaven,
from there I will bring them down.
If they hide themselves on the top of Carmel,
from there I will search them out and take them;
and if they hide from my sight at the bottom of the sea (*yām*),
there I will command the serpent, and it shall bite them.
And if they go into captivity before their enemies,
there I will command the sword, and it shall kill them;
and I will fix my eyes upon them
for evil and not for good.

Joel 2 describes the day of the Lord even more graphically:

Blow a trumpet in Zion;
sound an alarm on my holy mountain!
Let all the inhabitants of the land tremble,
for *the day of the Lord* is coming; it is near,
a day of darkness (*ḥōšek*) and gloom,
a day of clouds and thick darkness!

Like blackness there is spread upon the mountains
> a great and powerful people;

their like has never been before,
> nor will be again after them
> through the years of all generations.

Fire devours before them,
> and behind them a flame burns.

The land is like *the garden of Eden* [cosmos] before them,
> but behind them a *desolate wilderness* [chaos],
> and nothing escapes them. . . .

The earth quakes before them;
> the heavens tremble.

The sun and the moon are *darkened*,
> and the stars *withdraw their shining* [chaos].[56]

The LORD utters his voice
> before his army,

for his camp is exceedingly great;
> he who executes his word is powerful.

For *the day of the LORD* is great and very awesome;
> who can endure it? (Joel 2:1–3, 10–11)

THE LORD CONTROLS THE WIND, THE SEA, AND A GREAT FISH

The account of Jonah (c. 760 BC) shows that the Lord controls not only the wind and the sea but also a great fish. The Lord sent his prophet Jonah to Nineveh, the capital of Israel's enemy Assyria, to warn them about their evil ways and God's judgment. But Jonah disobeyed God's command and instead went in the opposite direction on a ship to Tarshish. "But the LORD hurled a great wind upon the

---

56. See Joel 2:31; 3:15: "The sun shall be turned to darkness, and the moon to blood, before the great and awesome day of the LORD comes. . . . The sun and the moon are darkened, and the stars withdraw their shining." See also Isaiah 13:10.

sea (*yām*), and there was a mighty tempest on the sea (*yām*), so that the ship threatened to break up" (Jonah 1:4).

When the mariners cast lots to see on whose account this evil had come upon them, "the lot fell on Jonah." Jonah confessed, "I am a Hebrew, and I fear the LORD, the God of heaven, who made the sea (*yām*) and the dry land. . . .' Then they said to him, 'What shall we do to you, that the sea (*yām*) may quiet down for us?' For the sea (*yām*) grew more and more tempestuous. He said to them, 'Pick me up and hurl me into the sea (*yām*); then the sea (*yām*) will quiet down for you, for I know it is because of me that this great tempest has come upon you. . . .' So they picked up Jonah and hurled him into the sea (*yām*), and the sea (*yām*) ceased from its raging. . . . And the LORD appointed a *great fish* to swallow up Jonah" (Jonah 1:7, 9, 11–12, 15, 17).

Jonah 2 continues:

Then Jonah prayed to the LORD his God from the belly of the fish, saying,

"I called out to the LORD, out of my distress,
     and he answered me;
out of the belly of *Sheol* [chaos] I cried,[57]
     and you heard my voice.
For you cast me into the *deep*,
     into the heart of the seas (*yāmmîm*),
     and the *flood* surrounded me [chaos];
all your waves and your billows
     passed over me.
Then I said, 'I am driven away
     from your sight;

---

57. "The psalmists often describe their experience of the absence of God, of God-forsakenness, as a descent into Sheol where there is no life precisely because in that dark region the 'shades' [ghosts] do not praise God." Anderson, *Creation Versus Chaos*, 95. See Psalms 18:4–5; 30:3; 42:7; 88:6–7.

yet I shall again look
    upon your holy temple.'[58]
The waters (*māyim*) closed in over me to take my life [chaos];
    the deep (*tĕhôm*) surrounded me;
weeds were wrapped about my head
    at the roots of the mountains.
I went down to the land
    whose bars closed upon me forever [chaos];
yet you brought up my life from the pit [cosmos],
    O LORD my God." (Jonah 2:1–6)

THE LORD CONTROLS THE RIVERS AND THE SEA

With probable allusions to the parting of the Red Sea (Ex. 14:21–29) and the drying up of the Jordan (Josh. 3:15–17), Habakkuk (c. 605 BC) speaks of the Lord controlling the rivers and the sea.

Was your wrath against the rivers, O LORD?
    Was your anger against the rivers,
        or your indignation against the sea (*yām*),
when you rode on your horses,
    on your chariot of *salvation*?
        . . . You split the earth with rivers.
The mountains saw you and writhed;
    the raging waters (*māyim*) swept on;
the deep (*tĕhôm*) gave forth its voice;
    it lifted its hands on high.
The sun and moon stood still in their place[59]

---

58. See Psalms 5:7 and 27:4: "But I, through the abundance of your steadfast love, will enter your house. I will bow down toward your holy temple in the fear of you"; "One thing have I asked of the LORD, that will I seek after: that I may dwell in the house of the LORD all the days of my life, to gaze upon the beauty of the LORD and to inquire in his temple."

59. "Probably an allusion to the victory at Gibeon (Jos 10:12–13), indicating that God's triumph over his enemies would be just as complete as on that occasion." *NIV Study Bible*, Habakkuk 3:11n.

at the light of your arrows as they sped,

at the flash of your glittering spear.

You marched through the earth in fury;

you threshed the nations in anger. [But the Lord's anger

was not just against the rivers and the sea (chaos);

his aim was to save his people and his anointed

king.]

You went out for the *salvation* of your people,

for the *salvation* of your anointed.

You crushed the head of the house of the wicked,

laying him bare from thigh to neck. *Selah*

You pierced with his own arrows the heads of his warriors,

who came like a whirlwind to scatter me,

rejoicing as if to devour the poor in secret.

You trampled the sea (*yām*) with your horses,

the surging of mighty waters (*māyim*) [an allusion to the

exodus]. (Hab. 3:8–15)

THE LORD REBUKES SATAN

Zechariah (c. 520 BC) received a vision of the high priest Joshua "clothed with filthy garments" (3:3) representing Israel's sins. "Then he showed me Joshua the high priest standing before the angel of the LORD, and *Satan* standing at his right hand *to accuse* him. And the LORD said to Satan, '*The LORD rebuke you, O Satan!* The LORD who has chosen Jerusalem *rebuke* you!'" (Zech. 3:1–2).

This is Satan, the serpent who tempted Adam and Eve in the garden to disobey the Lord and brought chaos into God's cosmos (Genesis 3). This is Satan, who tempted Job to curse God to his face (Job 2:5) and who tempted David to disobey the Lord by counting Israel's soldiers (1 Chron. 21:1). Satan here lives up to his name, "Accuser," in seeking to accuse the Lord's high priest and Israel for their sins. But the Lord outmaneuvers Satan. The Lord says, "Behold, I will bring my servant the Branch. . . . I will remove the iniquity of this land in a single day" (Zech. 3:8–9). That single day is Good Friday.

Questions for Reflection

1. What, according to the Minor Prophets, is "the day of the Lord"?

2. What will happen on the day of the Lord?

3. What is the day of the Lord in the New Testament? (See Acts 17:30–31; 1 Thess. 5:1–11.)

4. How does the account of Jonah reveal God's sovereignty over chaos?

5. Read Zechariah 3:1–4. Who is Satan? What is the meaning of the name *Satan*?

6. How did Satan originally cause chaos in this world?

7. Name some forms of chaos Satan causes today.

8. What is the meaning of the name *Joshua* (Zech. 3:1)? What is the Greek (New Testament) name for Joshua? (See Matt. 1:21.)

9. Who is the Lord's "servant, the Branch" of Zechariah 3:8? (See Isa. 11:1; 42:1–4; Jer. 23:5; 33:15; Phil. 2:5–7.)

10. Do you fear the day of the Lord? Why or why not?

Chaos–Cosmos in Daniel

We conclude our Old Testament overview with Daniel (605–535 BC) and his apocalyptic visions, especially those in chapters 7–12.

FOUR EVIL EMPIRES EMERGE FROM THE SEA

Daniel 7 records the vision of four beasts coming up out of the sea. The beasts represent four world empires, traditionally identified as Babylonia (605–539 BC), Medo-Persia (539–331 BC), Greece (331–63 BC), and Rome (63 BC–AD 476 and present).[60] These empires are clearly portrayed as evil: they come up out of the chaotic sea; they are not ordinary animals but hybrids, mutants; and their actions are evil. But then another figure appears, the Ancient of Days, who judges these evil empires. Daniel writes:

> In the first year of Belshazzar king of Babylon, Daniel saw a dream and visions of his head as he lay in his bed. Then he wrote down the dream and told the sum of the matter. Daniel declared, "I saw in my vision by night, and behold, the four *winds* of heaven were stirring up the great sea (*yammā*ʾ). And four great beasts came up out of the sea (*yammā*ʾ), different from one another. The first was like a lion and had eagles' wings. . . . And behold, another beast, a second one, like a bear. It was raised up on one side. It had three ribs in its mouth between its teeth; and it was told, 'Arise, *devour much flesh.*' After this I looked, and behold, another, like a leopard, with four wings of a bird on its back. And the beast had four heads, and dominion was given to it. After this I saw in the night visions, and behold, a fourth beast, *terrifying and dreadful* and exceedingly strong. It had *great iron teeth; it devoured and broke in pieces and stamped what was left with its feet* [chaos]. . . .

---

60. See my *Preaching Christ from Daniel*, 212–18.

"As I looked,
thrones were placed,
    and the Ancient of Days took his seat. . . .
the court sat in judgment,
    and the books were opened. . . .

"And as I looked, *the beast was killed*, and its body destroyed and given over to be burned with fire. As for the rest of the beasts, their *dominion was taken away*, but their lives were prolonged for a season and a time." (Dan. 7:1–7, 9–12)

A Son of Man Receives an Everlasting Kingdom

Daniel 7 continues:

I saw in the night visions,

and behold, with the clouds of heaven
    there came one like *a son of man*,
and he came to the Ancient of Days
    and was presented before him.
And to him was given dominion
    and glory and a kingdom,
*that all peoples, nations, and languages
    should serve him* [cosmos];
his dominion is an *everlasting dominion*,
    which shall not pass away,
and his kingdom one
    that shall not be destroyed [cosmos]. (Dan. 7:13–14)

Anderson observes, "In apocalyptic the whole historical drama, from creation to consummation, is viewed as a cosmic conflict between the divine and the demonic, creation and chaos, the kingdom of God and the kingdom of Satan. . . . Seen in this perspective, the role of the Anointed One, the Messiah, would be not just to liberate men from the bondage of sin but to battle triumphantly against the formidable powers of chaos."[61]

TRIBULATION, RESURRECTION FROM THE DEAD, AND EVERLASTING LIFE

In his final chapter, Daniel speaks of a time of tribulation, which will be followed by a resurrection from the dead: "At that time shall arise Michael, the great prince who has charge of your people. And there shall be *a time of trouble* [chaos], such as never has been since there was a nation till that time. But *at that time your people shall be delivered* [cosmos], everyone whose name shall be found written in the book. And many of *those who sleep in the dust of the earth shall awake, some to everlasting life* [cosmos], and some to shame and *everlasting contempt* [chaos]. And those who are wise *shall shine like the brightness of the sky above*; and those who turn many to righteousness, *like the stars forever and ever* [cosmos]"[62] (Dan. 12:1–3). In the end the light will overcome the darkness; orderly cosmos will replace chaos.

---

61. *Creation Versus Chaos*, 143.
62. Compare Matthew 13:43: "Then the righteous will shine like the sun in the kingdom of their Father."

Questions for Reflection

Daniel contains apocalyptic visions of the future similar to those in the book of Revelation (the Greek name for Revelation is *Apokalypsis*).

1. Daniel sees four beasts, representing four world empires, coming up *out of the sea*. What does this tell you about these world empires?

2. What descriptions about these beasts confirm this message?

3. What makes these empires evil? (See, e.g., Dan. 3:14–15; 7:1–12, 23–25; Jer. 51:34; Rev. 1:9.)

4. Who is the Ancient of Days? Why is he called "the Ancient of Days"?

5. What did "one like a son of man" receive?

6. In the New Testament who called himself "the Son of Man"? (See, e.g., Matt. 9:6; 24:27, 30, 37, 39, 44.) What does that title teach us about his mission?

7. Daniel 12:1 says that at the time of the end there shall be utter chaos: "There shall be a time of trouble, such as never has been since there was a nation till that time." How does the New Testament describe this time of trouble known as the "great tribulation"? (See Matt. 24:9–14, 21–22, 29–31; Rev. 7:13–14.)

8. Daniel 12:2 continues with the clearest Old Testament verse on the resurrection of the body: "And many [likely means "all"] of those who sleep in the dust of the earth shall awake, some to everlasting life, and some to shame and everlasting contempt." Who are "those who sleep in the dust of the earth"? Where does God say, "You are dust, and to dust you shall return"? According to Daniel 12:2, what happens to this form of chaos, death? (See also Rev. 21:4.)

9. What are the similarities between Daniel 12:2 and John 5:28–29? What are the differences?

10. Daniel 12:3 says, "And those who are wise shall shine like the brightness of the sky above; and those who turn many to righteousness, like the stars forever and ever." What are the similarities between these words and Matthew 13:43? What are the differences?

11. For those who believe in Jesus Christ, the chaos of death will turn into everlasting cosmos! Explain with New Testament passages.

Chapter 3

The Chaos–Cosmos Theme
in the New Testament

We have followed the chaos–cosmos theme in the Old Testament primarily by tracking the five Hebrew words identified in Genesis 1:2:

> The earth was without form and void (*tōhû wābōhû*), and darkness (*hōšek*) was over the face of the deep (*tĕhôm*). And the Spirit of God was hovering over the face of waters (*māyim*).

Genesis 1 adds two more words that refer to chaos: "Seas" (*yāmmîm*) in verse 10 and "sea creatures/monsters" (*tănnînim*) in verse 21. The Septuagint translated Genesis 1:2 as follows: "The earth was without form (*aoratos*) and void (*akataskeuastos*), and darkness (*skotos*) was over the face of the deep (*abyssou*). And the Spirit of God was hovering over the face of the waters (*hydatos*)." The Septuagint translated "seas" as *thalassas* and "great sea creatures/monsters" as *ta kētē ta megala*.

The New Testament uses some of these same words for chaos but it focuses especially on the contrast between darkness (*skotos*) and light (*phōs*) and various synonyms. Moreover, it centers the chaos–cosmos theme primarily in the battle between Satan, the Prince of Darkness,[1] and Jesus, "the light of the world" (John 8:12; 9:5). Another new element is that creation is viewed Christologically. Jesus Christ, the Word of God, is not only the maker of the first creation, which is now broken, but also the maker of the coming new creation. With Christ's first coming, the light began to penetrate the darkness, but there still remains much darkness (chaos) in this world. In terms of the light, this is the time of the "already" and the "not yet." It's like the dawn of a cloudless day: still somewhat dark but with the certain promise of full sunlight. Only at his second coming will the light (cosmos) completely displace the darkness.[2]

Chaos–Cosmos in the Gospels

Jesus, the Word of God, Is the Great Creator

John 1 echoes Genesis 1: "In the beginning." John also alludes to the ten times "God said" in Genesis 1 by calling Jesus the *Word* through whom all things were made. "In the beginning was the Word, and the Word was with God, and the Word was God. He was in the beginning with God. *All things* were made through him, and without him was not any thing made that was made" (John 1:1–3).[3] The implication is that it was through Christ that the primeval chaos of Genesis 1:2 came into being.

---

1. "The prince of the power of the air" (Eph. 2:2). See also 1 John 3:8: "The devil has been sinning from the beginning. The reason the Son of God appeared was to destroy the works of the devil."

2. "Disagreeing with Jewish apocalyptic visionaries, the early Christian community broke with the sharp separation between the two ages. These two ages are not like two circles that touch each other only tangentially; rather, the two circles overlap. For already in the old age the leaven of God's kingdom is at work; already in the time of the old creation a new creation is beginning." Anderson, *From Creation to New Creation*, 238.

3. See Prov. 8:22, 29–31: "The LORD possessed me [wisdom] at the beginning of his work, the first of his acts of old. . . . When he marked out the foundations of the earth, then I was beside him, like a master workman, and I was daily his delight, rejoicing before him always, rejoicing in his inhabited world and delighting in the children of man." See also Colossians 1:16–17: "For by him [Christ] all things were created, in heaven and on earth, visible and invisible, whether thrones or dominions or rulers or authorities—all things were created through him and for him. And he is before all things, and in him all things hold together."

GOD SO LOVED THE COSMOS

In John 3:16–17 Jesus declares, "For God so loved the world [*ton kosmon*, the orderly world God created in the beginning], that he gave his only Son, that whoever believes in him should not perish but have *eternal life*. For God did not send his Son into the world (*ton kosmon*) to condemn the world (*ton kosmon*), but in order that the world (*ho kosmos*) *might be saved* through him." In his first letter, John echoes Jesus's words: "In this the love of God was made manifest among us, that God sent his only Son into the world (*ton kosmon*), so that we might live through him" (1 John 4:9).

JESUS, THE LIGHT OF THE WORLD, SHINES IN THE DARKNESS

In the beginning God created light to drive back the darkness of chaos (Gen. 1:3–4). In the New Testament, Jesus at his first coming is pictured as the light that drives back the darkness of chaos at the microcosmic level. In describing the beginning of Jesus's ministry, Matthew quotes Isaiah 9:2: "The people dwelling in *darkness* have seen *a great light*, and for those dwelling in the region and shadow of *death*, on them *a light* has dawned" (Matt. 4:16). The parallelism indicates that darkness and death are synonyms, each referring to chaos. Matthew continues: "From that time Jesus began to preach, saying, 'Repent, for the *kingdom of heaven* is at hand'" (Matt. 4:17). Matthew links the dawning of the light with the kingdom of heaven (cosmos) being at hand.

John writes, "In him [the Word] was *life*, and the *life* was the *light* of men. The *light* shines in the darkness, and the *darkness* has not overcome it. . . . The true *light*, which gives *light* to everyone, was coming into the world" (John 1:4–5, 9). Jesus himself said, "I am the *light* of the world. Whoever follows me will not walk in *darkness* [chaos], but will have the *light* of life [cosmos]" (John 8:12).

Unfortunately, many people loved the darkness instead of the light. Jesus speaks of the judgment: "And this is the judgment: the light has come into the world, and people loved the darkness rather than the *light* because their works were *evil*. For everyone who does *wicked* things hates the *light* and does not come to the *light*, lest his works should be exposed. But whoever does what is true comes to the *light*, so that it may be clearly seen that his works have been carried out *in God*" (John 3:19–21).

Just before his death, Jesus warned the people, "The *light* is among you for a little while longer. Walk while you have the *light*, lest *darkness* overtake you. The one who walks in the *darkness* does not know where he is going. While you have the *light*, believe in the *light*, that you may become sons of *light*. . . . I have come into the world as *light*, so that whoever believes in me may not remain in *darkness* [chaos]" (John 12:35–36, 46).

Jesus Contrasts the Kingdom of Heaven with the Outer Darkness

One day a Roman centurion sent a message asking Jesus to heal his paralyzed, suffering servant. When Jesus came close to the centurion's house, the centurion sent friends with another message: "'Lord, I am not worthy to have you come under my roof, but only say the word, and my servant will be healed.' . . . When Jesus heard this, he marveled and said to those who followed him, 'Truly, I tell you, with no one in Israel have I found such faith. I tell you, many will come from east and west and recline at table with Abraham, Isaac, and Jacob in the *kingdom of heaven* [cosmos], while the sons of the kingdom will be thrown into the *outer darkness*. In that place there will be weeping and gnashing of teeth'" (Matt. 8:8, 10–12). The "outer darkness," similar to the Old Testament *Sheol*, the netherworld, is the chaos of hell.[4]

---

4. See also Matthew 22:13 and 25:30, 41: "Then the king said to the attendants, 'Bind him hand and foot and cast him into the *outer darkness*. In that place there will be weeping and

JESUS WITHSTANDS SATAN'S TEMPTATIONS

Immediately after John baptized Jesus, Satan tempted Jesus to terminate his road of suffering and to seek his own good instead.[5] Interestingly, the Spirit—not Satan—initiated this confrontation. The Spirit wanted Jesus to be tested just as Israel had been tested in the wilderness (Deut. 8:1–6). "Then Jesus was led up by the Spirit into the wilderness to be tempted by the *devil*." As the Devil tempted the first Adam by suggesting a way in which he could improve himself ("You will be like God" [Gen. 3:5]), so the Devil tempts Jesus to improve his lot. The first temptation is to still his hunger: "And after fasting forty days and forty nights, he was hungry. And the *tempter* came and said to him, 'If you are the Son of God, command these stones to become loaves of bread.' But he answered, 'It is written, "Man shall not live by bread alone, but by every word that comes from the mouth of God [Deut. 8:3]"'" (Matt. 4:1–4).

The second temptation is to become famous in an instant: "Then the *devil* took him to the holy city and set him on the pinnacle of the temple and said to him, 'If you are the Son of God, throw yourself down, for it is written, "He will command his angels concerning you," and "On their hands they will bear you up, lest you strike your foot against a stone."' Jesus said to him, 'Again it is written, "You shall not put the Lord your God to the test"'" (Matt. 4:5–7).

The third temptation is to become King of kings without suffering: "Again, the *devil* took him to a very high mountain and showed him *all the kingdoms of the world* and their glory. And he said to him, '*All these I will give you*, if you will fall down and worship me.' Then Jesus said to him, 'Be gone, *Satan*! For it is written, "You shall

---

gnashing of teeth."' "'Cast the worthless servant into *the outer darkness*. In that place there will be weeping and gnashing of teeth.' . . . Then he will say to those on his left, 'Depart from me, you cursed, into the eternal fire prepared for *the devil and his angels*.'".

5. Later, when Peter urged Jesus to terminate his road of suffering, Jesus "*rebuked* Peter and said, 'Get behind me, Satan! For you are not setting your mind on the things of God, but on the things of man'" (Mark 8:33).

worship the Lord your God and him only shall you serve."' Then the *devil* left him, and behold, angels came and were ministering to him" (Matt. 4:8–11).

By withstanding Satan's temptations, Jesus bound Satan; that is, he made Satan vulnerable to losing his followers. As Jesus explained in a short parable, "No one can enter a strong man's [Satan's] house and plunder his goods, unless he first *binds* the strong man. Then indeed he may plunder his house" (Mark 3:27). By resisting Satan's temptations, Jesus had bound Satan and could begin plundering Satan's house, freeing people from Satan's dominion by casting out demons. Orderly cosmos was overcoming chaos.

Jesus Rebukes Demons and Casts Them Out

According to Mark, Jesus began his ministry by proclaiming, "The time is fulfilled, and *the kingdom of God* is at hand; repent and believe in the gospel" (Mark 1:15). To demonstrate how near the kingdom of God, cosmos, had come with the coming of Jesus, Mark relates what happened when Jesus was teaching in the synagogue of Capernaum. "And immediately there was in their synagogue a man with an *unclean spirit* [chaos]. And he cried out, 'What have you to do with us, Jesus of Nazareth? *Have you come to destroy us?* I know who you are—the Holy One of God.' But Jesus *rebuked*[6] him, saying, 'Be silent, and come out of him!' And the *unclean spirit*, convulsing him and crying out with a loud voice, *came out of him*. And they were all amazed, so that they questioned among themselves, saying, 'What is

---

6. Anderson writes, "Howard C. Kee, 'The Terminology of Mark's Exorcism Stories' (unpublished) has drawn attention to the usage of the Greek verb *epitimaō*, which is often translated 'rebuke' in the exorcism stories of Mark, a verb that is found in several Qumran texts in its Semitic equivalent, *ga'ar*. This verb he traces back into the Old Testament where in a number of instances the text speaks of God's 'rebuke' of the waters of chaos (e.g., Pss. 18:16 [15]; 104:7; 106:9)." Anderson, *Creation Versus Chaos*, 162. See Isaiah 50:2: "Behold, by my rebuke I dry up the sea," and Zechariah 3:2: "And the LORD said to Satan, 'The LORD rebuke you, O Satan! The LORD who has chosen Jerusalem rebuke you!'" See also 2 Samuel 22:16 and Job 26:11–12.

this? A new teaching with authority! He commands even the *unclean spirits*, and they obey him'" (Mark 1:23–27).

Later a father brought his son to Jesus to be healed from an unclean spirit that "often cast him into fire and into water, *to destroy him* [chaos].... And when Jesus saw that a crowd came running together, he *rebuked the unclean spirit*, saying to it, 'You mute and deaf spirit, I command you, come out of him and never enter him again.' And after crying out and convulsing him terribly, it came out, and the boy was like a corpse, so that most of them said, 'He is dead [chaos].' But Jesus took him by the hand and lifted him up, and he arose [cosmos]" (Mark 9:22, 25–27).

On another occasion, "A *demon-oppressed man* who was blind and mute was brought to him, and he healed him, so that the man spoke and saw.... But when the Pharisees heard it, they said, 'It is only by *Beelzebul*, the prince of *demons*, that this man casts out *demons*.' Knowing their thoughts, he said to them, 'Every kingdom divided against itself is laid waste, and no city or house divided against itself will stand. And if *Satan* casts out Satan, he is divided against himself. How then will his kingdom stand?[7] ... But *if it is by the Spirit of God that I cast out demons* [chaos], *then the kingdom of God* [cosmos] *has come upon you*'" (Matt. 12:22–28).[8]

By casting out demons, Jesus undermined Satan's evil dominion. Later Jesus would send out seventy-two followers to "heal the sick

---

7. "Perhaps the major characteristic of New Testament demonology is the view that the demons are agents or manifestations of the *Evil One*, who is the head of the kingdom of evil. Evil is portrayed not as a plurality of haphazard forces but rather as an empire ruled by a single Power which . . . is personified as Satan. And over against the kingdom of evil, in fundamental and irreconcilable opposition to it, stands the kingdom of God. The Messiah, as portrayed in the Gospels, is the aggressor against Satan. By word and deed he precipitates the conflict and gives evidence of the final victory of God's kingdom, which is even now at hand." Anderson, *Creation Versus Chaos*, 150. Compare Cohn, "Exorcism, healing, telling of the kingdom—these were all ways of extricating people from the dominion of Satan." *Cosmos, Chaos and the World to Come*, 196.

8. See Peter's sermon in Acts 10:38: "God anointed Jesus of Nazareth with the Holy Spirit and with power. He went about doing good and healing [restoring cosmos] all who were *oppressed by the devil* [chaos], for God was with him."

. . . and say to them, 'The kingdom of God has come near to you.'"
Luke reports, "The seventy-two returned with joy, saying, 'Lord, even
the *demons* are subject to us in your name!' And he said to them, 'I
saw *Satan* fall like lightning from heaven'" (Luke 10:9, 17–18). Jesus
likens the healing of the sick and the nearness of the kingdom of
God to Satan falling from heaven.[9] With Jesus's first coming, Satan,
the personification of chaos, is losing his grip on his evil kingdom.

Jesus Rebukes the Wind and Calms the Sea

One evening Jesus and his disciples were crossing Lake Galilee in a
small boat. Suddenly a great storm arose, whipping up the waters.
The mighty waves crashed into the boat and filled it with water. The
disciples, who were experienced fishermen, were terrified. They woke
Jesus, who was asleep in the stern, and shouted at him, "'Teacher, do
you not care that we are perishing?' And [Jesus] awoke and *rebuked*
the wind and said to *the sea*, 'Peace! Be still!' And the wind ceased,
and there was a great calm. He said to them, 'Why are you so afraid?
Have you still no faith?' And they were filled with great fear and said
to one another, 'Who then is this, that even the wind and *the sea* obey
him?'" (Mark 4:38–41).[10]

Jesus "rebuked the wind, and said to the sea, 'Peace! Be still!'"
The word *rebuke* is also used in Psalm 104:7 of God in the beginning
rebuking the chaotic waters: "At your rebuke they [the waters] fled;
at the sound of your thunder they took to flight."[11] Who then is Jesus?

---

9. See John 12:31: "Now is the judgment of this world; now will the ruler of this world be
cast out." See also Revelation 12:7–9.

10. Compare Psalm 107:28–29: "Then they cried to the Lᴏʀᴅ in their trouble, and he deliv-
ered them from their distress. He made the storm be still, and the waves of the sea were hushed."
See also Job 9:8: "[God] alone stretched out the heavens and trampled the waves of the sea," and
Job 26:12: "By his power he [God] stilled the sea."

11. "The Greek verb translated 'rebuked' (*epitimaō*) is cognate with the noun 'rebuke'
(*epitimēsis*) that is used in Psalm 104:7 (103:7 LXX) to describe the action of the divine King in
quelling the chaotic sea at the time of Creation. Jesus is the divine King. His coming to establish
cosmic cosmos and bring abundant life was what the ancients and all of creation longed for (Pss.
96:10–13; 98:7–9)." Futato, *Interpreting the Psalms*, 180.

Jesus is the one who can turn chaos into orderly cosmos. The word *rebuke* is also used in Psalm 106:9: "He rebuked the Red Sea, and it became dry, and he led them through the deep as through a desert." Who then is Jesus? He is the one who can rebuke the sea and save his people.

Jesus Is Sovereign over the Chaotic Sea

Three Gospels report that Jesus walked on the sea.[12] The disciples were in a boat crossing the Sea of Galilee but made little headway because the wind was against them. During the fourth watch of the night (3:00–6:00 a.m.), Jesus "came to them, walking on *the sea*. He meant to pass by them, but when they saw him walking on *the sea* they thought it was a ghost, and cried out, for they all saw him and were terrified. But immediately he spoke to them and said, 'Take heart; *it is I*. Do not be afraid.' And he got into the boat with them, and *the wind ceased*. And they were utterly astounded, for they did not understand about the loaves, but their hearts were hardened" (Mark 6:48–52). Jesus identified himself as "it is I" (*egō eimi*), the same words by which God identified himself in Exodus 3:14, "I AM WHO I AM" (*egō eimi*, LXX), before saving Israel through the sea. Jesus's walking on the sea is a clear sign that he is sovereign over the chaotic sea.

Jesus's Power Heals the Sick

As we have seen, sickness and death are forms of chaos that resulted from the fall into sin. Jesus overcomes this chaos by restoring many sick people to good health. Luke reports on people "who came to hear him and to be healed of their diseases. And those who were troubled with *unclean spirits* were cured. And all the crowd sought to

---

12. Matthew 14:22–33; Mark 6:45–52; John 6:15–21.

touch him, for *power came out from him and healed them all*" (Luke 6:18–19). Later, crowds "followed him, and he welcomed them and spoke to them of the kingdom of God and *cured* those who had need of healing" (Luke 9:11).

The Roman centurion we met earlier believed that Jesus's word was so powerful that Jesus could heal his servant at a distance. The centurion said, "Lord, I am not worthy to have you come under my roof, but only say the word, and my servant will be healed." Jesus said, "Go; let it be done for you as you have *believed*." Matthew reports, "And the servant was *healed* at that *very moment*" (Matt. 8:8, 13). By healing those who suffered from illness and unclean spirits (chaos), Jesus showed that he had come into this world to restore cosmos.

JESUS RAISES THE DEAD

On another occasion, Jairus's young daughter was dying. Jairus begged Jesus to come to his house to heal her. But before they could get to the house, someone came and said to Jairus, "'Your daughter is *dead* [chaos]; do not trouble the Teacher any more.' But Jesus on hearing this answered him, 'Do not fear; only believe, and she will be *well*' [cosmos]. And when he came to the house . . . all were weeping and mourning for her, but he said, 'Do not weep, for she is not dead but sleeping.' And they laughed at him, knowing that she was *dead*. But taking her by the hand he called, saying, 'Child, arise.' And her *spirit returned*, and she got up at once. And he directed that something should be given her to eat" (Luke 8:49–55). Her life was normal again—an orderly cosmos.

For human beings, death is an ultimate form of chaos. But by resurrecting Jairus's daughter, Jesus demonstrated his sovereignty over death and his power to turn this ultimate form of chaos into orderly cosmos.

THE POWERS OF DARKNESS SEEK TO DESTROY JESUS

At the Last Supper Jesus was troubled and announced that one of the Twelve would betray him. When the disciples wanted to know who it was, "Jesus answered, 'It is he to whom I will give this morsel of bread when I have dipped it.' So when he had dipped the morsel, he gave it to Judas, the son of Simon Iscariot. Then after he had taken the morsel, *Satan entered into him*. Jesus said to him, 'What you are going to do, do quickly.' . . . So, after receiving the morsel of bread, he immediately went out. And it was night" (John 13:26–27, 30). It was *night*! In view of John's contrasts between light and darkness, "it was night" means more than that the sun had set. It was *dark*! Chaos! And it would get darker.

Later that night Judas sought to betray Jesus with a kiss. Jesus said to the chief priests and elders who had come out against him, "Have you come out as against a robber, with swords and clubs? When I was with you day after day in the temple, you did not lay hands on me. But this is your hour, and *the power of darkness*" (Luke 22:52–53). That is, in this your hour, darkness—chaos—has authority (*exousia tou skotous*).

The next day, when Jesus was crucified, from noon until three o'clock "there was *darkness* over the whole land . . . , while the sun's light failed" (Luke 23:44–45). The light of the world was dying, and creation reacted accordingly. It was a foretaste of the dark day of the Lord. To all appearances, the world was slipping back into chaos.

JESUS RISES FROM DEATH

Earlier, when the scribes and Pharisees had asked Jesus for a sign, he answered, "An evil and adulterous generation seeks for a sign, but no sign will be given to it except the sign of the prophet Jonah. For just as Jonah was three days and three nights in the belly of the great fish, so will the Son of Man be *three days and three nights in the heart of the earth*" (Matt. 12:39–40). Jesus interpreted Jonah's experience as a type that prefigured his upcoming experience. As Jonah descended into the chaotic sea for three days and three nights, so Jesus will descend into the chaos of death for three days and three nights. But this comparison also implies that just as Jonah escaped from the chaotic sea, so Jesus would escape from the chaos of death. Jesus added, however, "Behold, something greater than Jonah is here" (Matt. 12:41). Jonah would live but later die again; Jesus would live forevermore.

Another time when the Jews asked Jesus for a sign, he said, "Destroy this temple, and in three days I will raise it up" (John 2:19). Jesus was speaking of the temple of his body. People indeed destroyed Jesus's body when they crucified him, pierced his body, and buried him. But three days later he rose from the dead. "He has risen!" is the climax of Mark's short Gospel (Mark 16:6). In fact, all four Gospels were written because Jesus rose from the dead. The astonishing news is that Jesus the Lord is sovereign even over the chaos of death.

Questions for Reflection

1. Having become acquainted with the chaos–cosmos theme in the Old Testament, which narratives about Jesus do you now see with new eyes? How do you understand them differently than before?

2. List some of the forms of "darkness," chaos, mentioned in the Gospels.

3. List some of the forms of "light," orderly cosmos, mentioned in the Gospels.

4. What three temptations did Satan put before Jesus?

5. Explain Jesus's short parable about binding a strong man: "No one can enter a strong man's house and plunder his goods, unless he first binds the strong man. Then indeed he may plunder his house" (Mark 3:27). How did Jesus bind Satan? How did Jesus plunder Satan's house?

6. In Matthew 12:28 Jesus says, "But if it is by the Spirit of God that I cast out demons, then the kingdom of God has come upon you." How does this saying inform the chaos–cosmos theme?

7. When we read that Jesus "rebuked the wind" and calmed the sea (Mark 4:38–41), what Old Testament references come to mind? What does Jesus's calming of the sea say about Jesus?

8. When three Gospels report that Jesus was "walking on the sea," what was their message?

9. When Dr. Luke (8:49–55) reports that Jesus raised Jairus's daughter from the dead, what was his message?

10. All four Gospels were written because Jesus himself rose from the dead. What was the earth-shaking significance of Jesus's resurrection? See Genesis 3:19 and 1 Corinthians 15:17–26. What does Jesus's resurrection say about the chaos–cosmos theme? See 1 Corinthians 15:20–26, 51–58.

Chaos–Cosmos in Acts

JESUS SENDS THE HOLY SPIRIT TO REVERSE THE CHAOS OF BABEL

Just before Jesus's ascension into heaven, his disciples asked him, "Lord, will you at this time restore the kingdom to Israel?" They were eager to see the full restoration of God's kingdom in Israel. But Jesus said to them, "It is not for you to know times or seasons that the Father has fixed by his own authority. But you will receive power when the Holy Spirit has come upon you, and you will be my witnesses in Jerusalem and in all Judea and Samaria, and to the end of the earth" (Acts 1:6–8). God's kingdom would no longer be confined to Israel. It would spread "to the end of the earth."

In Acts 2:4–11 Luke reports that Jesus sent the promised Spirit on the day of Pentecost:

> And they were all filled with *the Holy Spirit* and began to speak in *other tongues* as the Spirit gave them utterance.
>
> Now there were dwelling in Jerusalem Jews, devout men *from every nation under heaven.* And at this sound the multitude came together, and they were bewildered, because *each one was hearing them speak in his own language.* And they were amazed and astonished, saying, "Are not all these who are speaking Galileans? And how is it that *we hear, each of us in his own native language?* Parthians and Medes and Elamites and residents of Mesopotamia, Judea and Cappadocia, Pontus and Asia, Phrygia and Pamphylia, Egypt and the parts of Libya belonging to Cyrene, and visitors from Rome, both Jews and proselytes, Cretans and Arabians—we hear them telling *in our own tongues* the mighty works of God."

The outpouring of the Spirit at Pentecost reversed for the early church the chaos of Babel. And the result was an amazing sense of unity in the church, even to sharing their possessions. "And all who believed were together and had *all things in common*. And they were selling their possessions and belongings and *distributing the proceeds to all, as any had need*. And day by day, attending the temple together and breaking bread in their homes, they received their food with glad and generous hearts, praising God and having favor with all the people. And the Lord added to their number day by day those who were being saved" (Acts 2:44–47). The church experienced a foretaste of Paradise (orderly cosmos) on earth.[13]

Jesus Commissions Paul to Spread the Light

Saul was on his way to Damascus to persecute Christians when the risen Lord Jesus stopped him. "Suddenly a *light* from heaven shone around him. And falling to the ground, he heard a voice saying to him, 'Saul, Saul, why are you persecuting me?' And he said, 'Who are you, Lord?' And he said, 'I am Jesus, whom you are persecuting'" (Acts 9:3–5). Persecution of God's people is a form of chaos similar to Israel being enslaved in Egypt.

Later, Paul testified to King Agrippa that the Lord Jesus himself had commissioned Paul to spread the light. The risen Lord had said to him, "Rise and stand upon your feet, for I have appeared to you for this purpose, to appoint you as a servant and witness to the things in which you have seen me and to those in which I will appear to you, delivering you from your people and from the Gentiles—to whom I am sending you to open their eyes, so that they may turn from *darkness* to *light* and *from the power of Satan* [chaos] *to God* [cosmos], that they may receive *forgiveness of sins* and a place among those who are *sanctified* by faith in me [cosmos]" (Acts 26:16–18).[14]

---

13. In Matthew 6 Jesus also taught his followers not to be anxious but to live as if paradise had already been restored: "Seek first the kingdom of God and his righteousness [cosmos], and all these things [food, drink, clothes] will be added to you" (Matt. 6:33).

14. Paul later writes about darkness and light: "At one time you were darkness, but now you are light in the Lord. Walk as children of light" (Eph. 5:8). See also Colossians 1:13: "He [the

JESUS HAD PREDICTED THE CHAOS OF PERSECUTION FOR HIS FOLLOWERS

The night before he died, Jesus prepared his followers for the chaos of persecution they would suffer. Jesus said, "If the world hates you, know that it has hated me before it hated you. . . . Remember the word that I said to you: 'A servant is not greater than his master.' If they *persecuted* me, they will also *persecute* you" (John 15:18, 20). And again, "I have said these things to you, that in me you may have *peace*. In the world you will have *tribulation* [chaos]. But take heart; *I have overcome the world*" (John 16:33).[15]

Jesus's followers will experience some form of tribulation in the world. This tribulation will intensify to the great tribulation just prior to Jesus's second coming. Jesus said, "Immediately after the *tribulation* of those days the *sun* will be *darkened*, and the *moon* will not give its *light*, and the *stars* will fall from heaven, and the powers of the heavens will be shaken [utter chaos].[16] Then will appear in heaven the sign of the Son of Man, and then all the tribes of the earth will mourn, and they will see *the Son of Man* [Jesus] coming on the clouds of heaven with *power and great glory*.[17] And he will send out his angels with a loud trumpet call, and they will gather his elect from the four winds, from one end of heaven to the other" (Matt. 24:29–31).

Father] has delivered us from the domain of darkness and transferred us to the kingdom of his beloved Son." And 2 Corinthians 4:6: "For God, who said, 'Let light shine out of darkness,' has shone in our hearts to give the light of the knowledge of the glory of God in the face of Jesus Christ."

15. In the Beatitudes Jesus said, "*Blessed* are those who are *persecuted* for righteousness' sake, for theirs is the kingdom of heaven. *Blessed* are you when others revile you and *persecute* you and utter all kinds of evil against you falsely on my account. Rejoice and be glad, for your reward is great in heaven . . ." (Matt. 5:10–12).

16. Jesus alludes to Joel 2:31: "The sun shall be turned to *darkness*, and the moon to blood, before the great and awesome day of the LORD comes." Peter used this passage in his sermon at Pentecost (see Acts 2:20). See also Joel 3:15; Isaiah 13:10; Ezekiel 32:7–8; Amos 8:9.

17. See Daniel 7:14: "And to him [one like a son of man] was given dominion and glory and a kingdom, that all peoples, nations, and languages should serve him; his dominion is an everlasting dominion, which shall not pass away, and his kingdom one that shall not be destroyed."

Questions for Reflection

1. Throughout church history people have tried to predict the date of Jesus's second coming. Some even quit their jobs and sold their homes as the predicted date came near. Can you share some recent examples? (Google "predictions for the second coming of Christ.")

2. Jesus's disciples also asked their risen Lord, "Lord, will you at this time restore the kingdom to Israel?" (Acts 1:6). What is wrong with their question? What is right about it?

3. What does Jesus's response to their question tell us about predicting the date of Jesus's return?

4. In Acts 2, Luke tells of the outpouring of the Holy Spirit on the day of Pentecost. List the three miracles that accompanied this first outpouring of the Holy Spirit.

5. Acts 2:4 says, "And they were all filled with the Holy Spirit and began to speak in other tongues as the Spirit gave them utterance." Have you ever heard people "speak in tongues"? Would you like to "speak in tongues"? Why or why not? See 1 Corinthians 12:7–11, 28–31; 13:1–8; 14:1–5, 12–13, 18–19.

6. At Pentecost, people from many different nations asked, "How is it that we hear, each of us in his own native language?" (Acts 2:8). What is the significance of different nationalities hearing the disciples speak in their "own native language"? See Genesis 11:1–9 and Revelation 7:9–10. What does this miracle say about the chaos–cosmos theme?

7. Luke reports that "all who believed were together and had all things in common. And they were selling their possessions and belongings and distributing the proceeds to all, as any had need" (Acts 2:44–45). What does this tell you about the chaos–cosmos theme? Should church members still have "all things in common"? Why or why not? If not, are we still obligated to help those in the church and beyond facing the chaos of hunger or homelessness? How?

8. In Acts 8:3 we read that "Saul was ravaging the church, and entering house after house, he dragged off men and women and committed them to prison." Explain how persecution is a form of chaos. How did the risen Christ turn Saul the persecutor into Paul the missionary?

9. Jesus predicted that his followers would suffer the chaos of persecution (e.g., John 15:20; 16:33). Can you share some statistics on the worldwide persecution of Christians? (Google "Persecution of Christians"). Have you suffered persecution? If so, how? See also 1 Corinthians 12:26.

10. Are you afraid of possible persecution? Can God use the chaos of persecution to bring about cosmos? See, for example, Matthew 5:10–12; Romans 8:35-39; 2 Corinthians 4:16–18; 2 Timothy 4:6–8. How will Jesus turn the chaos of persecution into cosmos? See, for example, Revelation 2:7, 10; 20:11–15.

Chaos–Cosmos in the Epistles

The New Testament Epistles continue the chaos–cosmos theme, especially in contrasting darkness and light, Satan and Christ, and in revealing that, through Christ's death and resurrection, God's curse of the creation (resulting in pain, suffering, and death) is partially lifted until this broken creation is fully restored to an orderly, harmonious cosmos at Christ's second coming.

ALL THINGS CREATED AND RECONCILED THROUGH CHRIST

Paul sets the overarching Christocentric tone concerning the chaos–cosmos theme in Colossians 1:15–20: "He [the Father's beloved Son] is the image of the invisible God, the firstborn of all creation. For *by him all things were created*, in heaven and on earth, visible and invisible, whether thrones or dominions or rulers or authorities—all things were *created through him and for him*.[18] And he is before all things, and *in him all things hold together*. And he is the head of the body, the church. He is the beginning, *the firstborn from the dead*, that in everything he might be preeminent. For in him all the fullness of God was pleased to dwell, and *through him to reconcile to himself all things*, whether *on earth or in heaven*, making *peace* by the blood of his cross." Through Jesus's blood shed on the cross orderly cosmos will be restored.

WE ARE CHILDREN OF THE LIGHT, DELIVERED FROM DARKNESS

In 2 Corinthians 4:6 Paul connects the original light that dispelled the darkness (Gen. 1:3) to Jesus Christ and Christians: "For God, who said, 'Let *light* shine out of *darkness*,' has shone in our hearts to give the *light of the knowledge of the glory of God in the face of Jesus Christ*."

---

18. Even thrones, dominions, rulers, and authorities that have turned evil (see Eph. 6:12) were created good by Christ (see Gen. 1:10, where God called the Seas "good").

In Ephesians 5:8–14 Paul adds, "For at one time you were *darkness*, but now you are *light* in the Lord.[19] Walk as children of *light* (for the fruit of *light* is found in all that is good and right and true), and try to discern what is pleasing to the Lord. Take no part in the unfruitful works of *darkness*, but instead expose them. . . . When anything is exposed by the *light*, it becomes visible, for anything that becomes visible is *light*. Therefore it says, 'Awake, O sleeper, and arise from the *dead*, and *Christ will shine on you*.'"

In Colossians 1:12–14 Paul writes that the Father "has qualified you to share in the inheritance of the saints in *light*. He has delivered us from *the domain of darkness* and transferred us to *the kingdom of his beloved Son*, in whom we have *redemption*, the *forgiveness of sins*."[20] Transferred from the kingdom of darkness into the kingdom of Jesus Christ, the light of the world, we are children of the light.

We Battle the Cosmic Powers of Darkness

The Epistles portray the Christian life as a battle against the dark forces of evil—chaos frequently being personified as the Devil or Satan. Peter urges the early Christians, "Be sober-minded; be watchful. Your *adversary the devil* prowls around like a roaring lion, seeking someone to *devour*" (1 Pet. 5:8).

Paul writes to the Romans: "The *night* is far gone; the *day* is at hand. So then let us cast off the works of *darkness* and put on the *armor of light*" (Rom. 13:12). Later Paul urges the Christians in Ephesus, "Put on the whole *armor of God*, that you may be able to stand

---

19. Collating parts of Exodus 19:6 and Deuteronomy 7:6, 10:15 as his basis, Peter writes to the early church, "But you are a chosen race, a royal priesthood, a holy nation, a people for his own possession, that you may proclaim the excellencies of him who called you out of darkness (*skotous*) into his marvelous light (*phōs*)" (1 Pet. 2:9).

20. Paul writes to the Thessalonians: "For you are all children of *light*, children of the *day*. We are *not of the night or of the darkness*" (1 Thess. 5:5).

against the schemes of the *devil*. For we do not wrestle against flesh and blood, but against the rulers, against the authorities, against the *cosmic powers* over this present *darkness*, against the *spiritual forces of evil in the heavenly places*" (Eph. 6:11–12).

THE CHAOS OF PRESENT SUFFERING AND THE HOPE OF A NEW CREATION

Paul makes it clear that the present chaos of suffering and death east of Eden is the result of human sin: "Therefore, just as *sin* came into the world *through one man*, and *death through sin*, and *so death spread to all men because all sinned*" (Rom. 5:12).

But Paul also looks beyond the present chaos of suffering and death to the cosmos of the new creation freed from its bondage to decay:

> For I consider that *the sufferings of this present time* are not worth comparing with the *glory* that is to be revealed to us. For *the creation* waits with eager longing for the revealing of the sons of God [in the new age]. For *the creation was subjected to futility* [Gen. 3:14–19], not willingly, but because of him [God] who subjected it, in hope [Gen. 3:15] that *the creation* itself will be set free from *its bondage to corruption* and obtain *the freedom of the glory of the children of God*. For we know that *the whole creation has been groaning together in the pains of childbirth* until now.[21] And not only *the creation*, but we ourselves, who have the firstfruits of the Spirit, *groan inwardly* as we wait eagerly for adoption as sons, the *redemption [resurrection] of our bodies*. (Rom. 8:18–23)

---

21. Paul personifies creation and views the chaos of present suffering as birth pangs leading to a new, restored creation. Peter writes, "But according to his promise we are waiting for new heavens and a new earth in which righteousness dwells" (2 Pet. 3:13). And John: "Then I saw a new heaven and a new earth, for the first heaven and the first earth had passed away" (Rev. 21:1).

In the Midst of Chaos We Are More than Conquerors

But suffering, groaning Christians have more than hope for a new creation. Even in the midst of our present suffering we are comforted by the love of Christ that remains with us. Paul asks, "Who shall separate us from the love of Christ? Shall *tribulation, or distress, or persecution, or famine, or nakedness, or danger, or sword* [all forms of chaos]? As it is written [in Ps. 44:22], 'For your sake we are being *killed* all the day long; we are regarded as sheep to be *slaughtered*.' No, *in all these things* we are *more than conquerors* through him who loved us. For I am sure that *neither death* nor life, *nor angels nor* [evil[22]] *rulers*, nor things present nor things to come, *nor* [evil] *powers*, nor height nor depth, nor anything else in all creation, will be able to separate us from the love of God in Christ Jesus our Lord" (Rom. 8:35–39). Since no form of chaos will be able to separate us from the love of God in Christ Jesus, we are more than conquerors, even in our suffering.

In Christ We Are Already a New Creation

The new creation for which we are waiting is already making inroads into the present chaos. Paul states it plainly: "If anyone is in Christ, he is *a new creation*. The old has passed away; behold, the *new has come*. All this is from God, who through Christ reconciled us to himself and gave us the ministry of reconciliation; that is, in Christ God was reconciling *the world* to himself, *not counting their trespasses against them*" (2 Cor. 5:17–19).[23]

John uses this tension between the already of the new creation

---

22. "For we do not wrestle against flesh and blood, but against the rulers, against the authorities, against the cosmic powers over this present *darkness*, against the spiritual forces of *evil* in the heavenly places" (Eph. 6:12).

23. "Thus it is written, 'The first man Adam became a living being'; the last Adam became a life-giving spirit" (1 Cor. 15:45).

(cosmos) and the not yet (chaos) to admonish his readers: "This is the message we have heard from him and proclaim to you, that God is *light*, and in him is *no darkness* [chaos] at all. If we say we have fellowship with him while we walk in *darkness*, we lie and do not practice the truth" (1 John 1:5–6). And again he warns: "It is a new commandment that I am writing to you, which is true in him and in you, because the *darkness* [chaos] is passing away and the true *light* [cosmos] is already shining. Whoever says he is in the *light* and hates his brother is still in *darkness*. Whoever loves his brother abides in the *light*, and in him there is no cause for stumbling. But whoever hates his brother is in the *darkness* and walks in the *darkness*, and does not know where he is going, because the *darkness* has blinded his eyes" (1 John 2:8–11).

John accentuates a lot of darkness in his warning. But the good news is that "the *darkness* [chaos] is passing away and the true *light* [cosmos] is already shining." And "whoever loves his brother abides in the *light* [cosmos]." In Christ we are already a new creation.

THE LAST DAYS ARE ALREADY HERE

John warns the early Christians that they live in the last days: "Children, it is the *last hour*, and as you have heard that *antichrist* is coming, so now many *antichrists have come*. Therefore we know that it is the *last hour*" (1 John 2:18). The antichrist is a rival Christ, a personification of chaos. John argues that so many people are denying that Jesus is the Christ,[24] that it must be the last hour—which means that Christ can return any time. Be prepared, therefore, for Christ's second coming!

In contrast, Paul had to correct the false belief in Thessalonica that Christ had *already* come. He writes in 2 Thessalonians 2:1–10:

---

24. "Who is the liar but he who denies that Jesus is the Christ? This is the antichrist, he who denies the Father and the Son" (1 John 2:22).

Now concerning *the coming of our Lord Jesus Christ* and our being gathered together to him, we ask you, brothers, not to be quickly shaken in mind or *alarmed*,[25] either by a spirit or a spoken word, or a letter seeming to be from us [a forged letter], to the effect that *the day of the Lord has come.* Let no one deceive you in any way. For *that day* will not come, unless *the rebellion comes first*, and *the man of lawlessness* [a personification of chaos] is revealed, the son of *destruction*, who *opposes* and *exalts himself against every so-called god*[26] or object of worship, so that he *takes his seat in the temple of God, proclaiming himself to be God.* Do you not remember that when I was still with you I told you these things? And you know what is restraining him now[27] so that he may be revealed in his time. For the *mystery of lawlessness* [chaos] *is already at work.* Only he who now restrains it will do so until he is out of the way.[28] And then *the lawless one* [chaos] will be revealed, *whom the Lord Jesus will kill with the breath of his mouth* and bring to nothing by the appearance of his coming. The coming of *the lawless one* is by the activity of *Satan* with all power and false signs and wonders,

25. Paul uses the same verb Jesus used when he cautioned, "And when you hear of wars and rumors of wars, do not be *alarmed*. This must take place, but the end is not yet" (Mark 13:7).

26. See Daniel 11:36: "And the king shall do as he wills. *He shall exalt himself and magnify himself above every god*, and shall speak astonishing things against the God of gods." At verse 36 Daniel moves from the evil king Antiochus IV (vv. 21–35) to the most evil end time king, the Antichrist. Antiochus IV never exalted himself and magnified himself above every god. In fact, he worshiped the Greek pantheon. See my *Preaching Christ from Daniel*, 357–58, 384–91.

27. The archangel Michael was known as "the protector of God's people" (Dan. 12:1, NRSV; see also Dan. 10:13, 20–21). See my *Preaching Christ from Daniel*, 356. Jeffrey A. D. Weima, in *1–2 Thessalonians*, Baker Exegetical Commentary on the New Testament (Grand Rapids, MI, 2014), 567–77, discusses seven different proposals identifying the restraining thing/person. I agree with him that the archangel Michael is the most compelling on the basis of Daniel 10–12 and its chronological schema, which Paul seems to follow in 2 Thessalonians 2:3–12. (1) Michael restrains evil (Dan. 10:20–11:45; 2 Thess. 2:6, 7). (2) Michael will stand aside (Dan. 12:1, see next note; 2 Thess. 2:7). (3) Unequaled tribulation (Dan. 12:1; 2 Thess. 2:3–4, 8–10). (4) The final judgment, God's people delivered, their enemies punished (Dan. 12:1–3; 2 Thess. 2:3–14). For more details, see Weima, *1–2 Thessalonians*, 506–42 and 576.

28. "The key verse is [Dan.] 12:1a, where Michael is said to 'stand' (MT) or, as rendered in the LXX, 'stand aside, pass by' (. . . , *parerchomai*)." Weima, *1–2 Thessalonians*, 576.

and with all wicked deception for those who are perishing, because they refused to love the truth and so be saved.

The point is that "the mystery of lawlessness [chaos] is already at work." We see forms of chaos all around us. We live in the last days. Christ can return at any time. Therefore we need to be prepared.

SATAN AND HIS FOLLOWERS WILL BE CAST INTO UTTER DARKNESS

In his ministry, Paul certainly experienced the opposition of Satan. For example, he wanted to go to Thessalonica: "I, Paul, again and again—but *Satan* hindered us" (1 Thess. 2:18). However, Paul confidently signs off his epistle to the Romans, "The God of peace will soon crush *Satan* under your feet. The grace of our Lord Jesus Christ be with you" (Rom. 16:20; see Gen. 3:15). The orderly cosmos will soon overcome disordered chaos.

Peter warns the church of the judgment to come:

For if God did not spare angels when they sinned, but cast them into *hell* [chaos] and committed them to chains of gloomy *darkness* to be kept until the judgment; if he did not spare the ancient world, but preserved [cosmos] Noah, a herald of righteousness, with seven others, when he brought a flood [chaos] upon the world of the ungodly; . . . then the Lord knows how to rescue [cosmos] the godly from trials, and to keep the unrighteous under punishment until the day of judgment, and especially those who indulge in the lust of defiling passion and despise authority. . . . These [false teachers] are waterless springs [deceivers] and mists driven by a storm [worthless]. For them the gloom of *utter darkness* [chaos] has been reserved. (2 Pet. 2:4–5, 9–10, 17).

Jude also speaks of the judgment to come both for devils and ungodly people. Jude writes, "And the angels who did not stay within their own position of authority, but left their proper dwelling, he has kept in eternal chains under gloomy *darkness* [chaos] until the judgment of the great day [the final judgment]" (v. 6).

"Ungodly people, who pervert the grace of our God into sensuality and deny our only Master and Lord, Jesus Christ" will also be condemned. "These are hidden reefs at your love feasts, as they feast with you without fear, shepherds feeding themselves; waterless clouds, swept along by winds; fruitless trees in late autumn, twice dead, uprooted; wild waves of *the sea*, casting up the foam of their own shame; wandering stars, for whom the gloom of *utter darkness* [chaos] has been reserved forever" (Jude 4, 12–13). Satan and his followers will be cast into "utter darkness," that is, the chaos of hell.

THE RESURRECTION FROM THE DEAD

Through the resurrection of Christ, death, an ultimate form of chaos, has been conquered. Paul teaches that we experience a foretaste of the resurrection today because even though our bodies are subject to death, our spirits are not. Paul writes, "But if Christ is in you, although the body is dead [chaos] because of sin, the Spirit is life because of righteousness.[29] If the Spirit of him who raised Jesus from the dead dwells in you, he who raised Christ Jesus from the dead will also give *life* [cosmos] to your mortal bodies through his Spirit who dwells in you" (Rom. 8:10–11).[30]

In 1 Corinthians 15 Paul elaborates on the resurrection of the body: "In fact Christ has been *raised from the dead*, the *firstfruits* of those who have fallen asleep. For as by a man came *death* [chaos],

---

29. An alternate reading is "yet your spirit is alive." Although the context of verse 11 favors "Spirit," verse 10 by itself favors the merism body–spirit.

30. See also 2 Timothy 1:10, ". . . our Savior Christ Jesus, who abolished death and brought life and immortality to light through the gospel."

by a man has come also the *resurrection of the dead* [cosmos]. For as *in Adam all die* [chaos], so also *in Christ shall all be made alive* [cosmos]. But each in his own order: Christ the firstfruits, then at his coming those who belong to Christ. Then comes the end, when he delivers the kingdom to God the Father after destroying every rule and every authority and power. For he must reign until he has put *all his enemies* [forms of chaos] under his feet. The last enemy to be destroyed is death" (1 Cor. 15:20–26).

Bernhard Anderson comments, "Here the ancient theme of the conflict with the powers of chaos is pitched in a new key. The victory of the King is transposed out of the realm of mythology into the realm of history where men of faith celebrate the Event which emancipates them from all forms of bondage and enables them to walk in newness of life."[31]

Paul continues in 1 Corinthians 15:

Behold! I tell you a mystery. We shall not all sleep, but we shall all be changed, in a moment, in the twinkling of an eye, at the last trumpet. For the trumpet will sound, and *the dead will be raised imperishable* [restored cosmos], and we shall be changed. For this *perishable* body must put on the *imperishable*, and this *mortal* body must put on *immortality*. When the *perishable* puts on the *imperishable*, and the *mortal* puts on *immortality* [cosmos] , then shall come to pass the saying that is written: 'Death is swallowed up in victory.' 'O death, where is your victory? O death, where is your sting?'[32] The sting of death is sin, and the power of sin is the law. But thanks be to God, who *gives us the victory through our Lord Jesus Christ*. (1 Cor. 15:51–57)

---

31. Anderson, *Creation Versus Chaos*, 176.
32. See Hosea 13:14: "I shall ransom them from the power of Sheol; I shall redeem them from Death. O Death, where are your plagues? O Sheol, where is your sting?"

Victory even over death itself! The words "perishable body" and "mortal body" signal chaos. By contrast the words "imperishable" and "immortality" signal orderly cosmos. The good news Paul may bring is that through the Lord Jesus Christ the curse of death (Gen. 3:19) will be lifted and we will gain the victory even over the chaos of death.

We Await a New Heavens and a New Earth

Peter had to confront scoffers who asked, "Where is the promise of his coming? For ever since the fathers fell asleep, all things are continuing as they were from the beginning of creation." Peter responds:

> They deliberately overlook this fact, that the heavens existed long ago, and the earth was formed out of water and through water by the word of God [Gen. 1:6–10], and that by means of these the world that then existed was deluged with water and perished [chaos, Genesis 7]. But by the same word the heavens and earth that now exist are stored up for fire, being kept until the day of judgment and destruction of the ungodly. . . . The Lord is not slow to fulfill his promise as some count slowness, but is patient toward you, not wishing that any should perish, but that all should reach repentance. . . . But according to his promise we are waiting for new heavens and a new earth in which righteousness dwells. (2 Pet. 3:4–7, 9, 13)[33]

That is our ultimate hope in this chaotic world: "We are waiting for *new heavens and a new earth* in which righteousness dwells."

---

33. See Isaiah 65:17; 66:22; Revelation 21:1.

Questions for Reflection

1. List the forms of chaos mentioned in the Epistles.

2. List the forms of cosmos mentioned in the Epistles.

3. The Epistles claim that the Christian life is a battle "against the cosmic powers over this present darkness" (Eph. 6:12). Explain. How did Paul experience this battle?

4. How do Christians today experience this battle? How have you experienced this battle? How can we possibly win this battle? (See 2 Cor. 5:17–21.)

5. How do we know that we live in the last days? Name two things that must happen before Christ returns.

6. List the forms of chaos Paul mentions in Romans 8:35. How can Paul say, "In all these things [in all these forms of chaos] we are more than conquerors" (Rom. 8:37)?

7. What is the already/not yet dynamic of cosmos today? How do we experience the "already" of cosmos today? How do we experience the "not yet" of cosmos today?

8. What is the last form of chaos to be destroyed?

9. How are you comforted by the teaching of the resurrection from the dead?

10. Second Peter 3:13 says, "But according to his promise we are waiting for new heavens and a new earth in which righteousness dwells." Are you longing for the fulfillment of this promise? Why or why not?

Chaos–Cosmos in Revelation 1–19

The book of Revelation (*Apokalypsis*) heightens the chaos–cosmos theme by using apocalyptic language like Daniel. Anderson characterizes the apocalyptic vision well: "In apocalyptic the whole historical drama, from creation to consummation, is viewed as a cosmic conflict between the divine and the demonic, creation and chaos, the kingdom of God and the kingdom of Satan. According to this view, the outcome will be God's victorious annihilation of the powers which threaten his creation, including death which apocalyptic writers regarded as an enemy hostile to God (Isa 25:8 . . .). Seen in this perspective, the role of the Anointed One, the Messiah, would be not just to liberate men from the bondage of sin but to battle triumphantly against the formidable powers of chaos."[34]

The Protagonist: One Like a Son of Man

According to Revelation 1, an angel gave John "the revelation of *Jesus Christ*" about "the things that must soon take place." He begins with a blessing for the seven churches in Asia: "Grace to you and peace from him who is and who was and who is to come, and from the *seven spirits* who are before his throne, and from *Jesus Christ* the faithful witness, the *firstborn of the dead*, and the ruler of kings on earth" (Rev. 1:1, 4–5).[35]

John describes himself as "your brother and partner in the *tribulation* (chaos) and the kingdom and the patient endurance that are in Jesus" (Rev. 1:9). But in contrast to the chaos of tribulation around him, he finds himself "*in the Spirit* on the Lord's day, and I heard behind me a loud voice like a trumpet" (Rev. 1:10). Being "in the Spirit," he experienced a form of cosmos in the midst of chaos. "The

---

34. Anderson, *Creation Versus Chaos*, 143.
35. "Seven" represents a complete number; "the firstborn of the dead" is the first conqueror of the chaos of death. See Colossians 1:18.

voice spoke: the saint turned: the Mediterranean island scene faded behind him, and before him opened the vision of another reality altogether"[36]: the risen, glorified Christ in the midst of his churches.

"Then I turned to see the voice that was speaking to me, and on turning I saw seven golden lampstands [the seven churches; 1:20], and in the midst of the lampstands *one like a son of man*,[37] clothed with a long robe and with a golden sash around his chest [like the high priests in the Old Testament]. . . . In his right hand he held seven stars [the complete number of churches], from his mouth came a sharp two-edged sword,[38] and his face was *like the sun shining in full strength*" (Rev. 1:12–13, 16). Here we have the light [cosmos] that dispelled the darkness of chaos in the beginning (Gen. 1:3). Here we see God: "God is light, and in him is no darkness at all" (1 John 1:5). Here we see Jesus, who said, "I am the light of the world" (John 8:12).

The Antagonist: Satan

In Revelation 2 John identifies the antagonist: Satan, the Prince of Darkness.[39] Following the light of the world does not mean escape

---

36. Michael Wilcock, *I Saw Heaven Opened: The Message of Revelation* (Downers Grove, IL: InterVarsity Press, 1975), 40.

37. See Daniel 7:13–14: "I saw in the night visions, and behold, with the clouds of heaven there came *one like a son of man*, and he came to the Ancient of Days and was presented before him. And to him was given *dominion* and *glory* and a *kingdom*, that all peoples, nations, and languages should serve him; his dominion is an everlasting dominion, which shall not pass away, and his kingdom one that shall not be destroyed."

38. The sword is his word of judgment. See Isaiah 11:4: "But with righteousness he shall judge the poor, and decide with equity for the meek of the earth; and he shall strike the earth with *the rod of his mouth*, and with the breath of his lips he shall kill the wicked." See also Hebrews 4:12: "For the word of God is living and active, *sharper than any two-edged sword*, piercing to the division of soul and of spirit, of joints and of marrow, and discerning the thoughts and intentions of the heart," and Revelation 19:15 regarding the rider of the white horse: "From his mouth comes a *sharp sword* with which to strike down the nations, and he will rule them with *a rod of iron*."

39. "In apocalyptic eschatology Satan was conceived as the leader of a history-long rebellion which in the last day will be completely quelled. Satan, therefore, is subordinate to God, and will ultimately be destroyed. His authority is limited to 'the present age,' when men experience both the 'already' and the 'not yet' of God's victory in the conflict of history. God has given him

from the forces of chaos.[40] Jesus instructs John to write to the angel of the church in Smyrna:

> The words of the first and the last, who died and came to life [the risen Christ]. "I know your *tribulation* and your poverty[41] (but you are rich) and the slander of those who say that they are Jews and are not, but are a synagogue of *Satan*. Do not fear what you are about to suffer. Behold, the *devil* is about to throw some of you into prison, that you may be tested, and for ten days [a full number of days] you will have *tribulation*. Be faithful unto *death* [chaos], and I will give you the crown of *life* [cosmos]. He who has an ear, let him hear what the Spirit says to the churches. The one who conquers will not be hurt by the *second death*.[42]" (Rev. 2:8–11)

Even though Christians may suffer unto death (physical death), they cannot be hurt by the second death, the lake of *fire*. Compared to a lake of water (chaos), the lake of fire, hell, which Jesus called "the *outer darkness*," will be the ultimate form of chaos.[43]

THE CHAOS OF LANGUAGES AT BABEL
REVERSED INTO COSMOS

Zephaniah prophesied that the Lord would reverse the chaos of languages at Babel into cosmos: "For at that time I will change

---

only a limited amount of rope, so to speak, and he cannot go beyond the bounds." Anderson, *Creation Versus Chaos*, 165.

40. See Jesus's predictions of persecution in Matthew 5:10–11 and John 15:20; 16:33. See also Paul's words, "Indeed, all who desire to live a godly life in Christ Jesus will be persecuted" (2 Tim. 3:12).

41. See Hebrews 10:34: "You joyfully accepted the *plundering of your property*, since you knew that you yourselves had a better possession and an abiding one."

42. See Revelation 20:14: "This is the second death, the lake of fire." See also Revelation 21:8: "But as for the cowardly, the faithless, the detestable, as for murderers, the sexually immoral, sorcerers, idolaters, and all liars, their portion will be in the lake that burns with fire and sulfur, which is *the second death*."

43. See Matthew 8:12; 22:13; 25:30.

the speech of the peoples to a *pure speech*, that all of them may call upon the name of the LORD and *serve him with one accord*" (Zeph. 3:9). This prophecy was temporarily fulfilled at Pentecost when Christians from various nations and languages could understand each other and served the Lord with one accord (Acts 2:5–11, 42–47). That unity was a foretaste of the unity God's people experience in heaven.

In Revelation 7 John writes, "After this I looked, and behold, a great multitude that no one could number, from *every nation, from all tribes and peoples and languages*, standing before the throne and before the Lamb, clothed in white robes, with palm branches in their hands, and crying out with a loud voice, 'Salvation belongs to our God who sits on the throne, and to the Lamb!'" (Rev. 7:9–10).[44]

Since God in heaven lifts the Babel curse of many languages, this unity is a harbinger of the perfect communication in the new heavens and earth that Christ will usher in with his second coming. In the new creation the chaos of Babel will be completely reversed into a cosmos of unity.

A GREAT RED DRAGON THREATENS THE MESSIAH AND THE CHURCH

John writes in Revelation 12:

> And a great sign appeared in heaven: a woman [Israel] clothed with the sun, with the moon under her feet, and on her head a crown of twelve stars [the twelve tribes of Israel]. She was pregnant and was crying out in birth pains and the agony of giving birth [to the Messiah]. And another

---

44. They stood before the Lamb (Jesus Christ), "clothed in white robes" (sinless) and washed "in the blood of the Lamb" (Rev. 7:13–14), waving a symbol of victory: palm branches.

sign appeared in heaven: behold, a great red *dragon*,[45] with *seven* heads[46] and *ten* horns,[47] and on his heads *seven* diadems.[48] His tail swept down a third of the *stars of heaven*[49] and cast them to the earth. And the *dragon* stood before the woman who was about to give birth, so that when she bore her child he might devour it. She gave birth to *a male child* [the Messiah], *one who is to rule all the nations with a rod of iron*,[50] but her *child was caught up to God and to his throne* [Jesus's ascension to heaven], and the woman fled into the *wilderness*,[51] where she has a place prepared by God, in which she is to be *nourished* for *1,260 days*. (Rev. 12:1–6)

John speaks here of the gospel age from Jesus's first coming to just prior to his second coming, the church age, the age we live in right now. There is worldwide persecution of the church; the number of Christian martyrs in the twentieth century has

---

45. Used nine times in Revelation for Satan, the Old Testament Leviathan. *"Drakōn*, 'dragon,' is the usual Septuagint rendering of Leviathan. Only once is Leviathan translated *kētos*, 'seamonster' (Job 3:8)." Wallace, "Leviathan and the Beast in Revelation," 67.

46. Seven kings. See Revelation 17:9–10: "This calls for a mind with wisdom: the seven heads are seven mountains on which the woman is seated; they are also seven kings."

47. Ten future kings. See Revelation 17:12: "And the ten horns that you saw are ten kings who have not yet received royal power." In light of Daniel the "ten horns" could also mean "exceedingly strong": "After this I saw in the night visions, and behold, a fourth beast, terrifying and dreadful and *exceedingly strong*. . . . It had *ten horns*" (Dan. 7:7).

48. The seven diadems represent complete authority. See Luke 4:5–7: "And the devil took him up and showed him all the kingdoms of the world in a moment of time, and said to him, 'To you I will give all this authority and their glory, for it has been delivered to me, and I give it to whom I will. If you, then, will worship me, it will all be yours.'"

49. "With its tail the dragon attacks the stars, those supreme symbols and guardians of the divinely appointed order, and flings a third of them down from their proper places on to the earth." Cohn, *Cosmos, Chaos and the World to Come*, 214.

50. The male child is the Messiah, the Son of God. See Revelation 19:15–16 regarding the rider on the white horse: "From his mouth comes a sharp sword with which to strike down the nations, and he will rule them with *a rod of iron*. . . . On his robe and on his thigh he has a name written, King of kings and Lord of lords." See Psalm 2:7–9: "I will tell of the decree: The LORD said to me, 'You are my Son; today I have begotten you. Ask of me, and I will make the nations your heritage, and the ends of the earth your possession. You shall break them with *a rod of iron*.'" See also Isaiah 11:4 and Hebrews 4:12.

51. The wilderness is a place of refuge. See Hosea 2:14: "Therefore, behold, I will allure her [Israel], and bring her into the *wilderness*, and speak *tenderly* to her."

been estimated at 45 million (chaos).[52] But amazingly, the Christian church on earth continues to thrive (cosmos in the midst of chaos). God continues to nourish his church throughout these last days.

WAR IN HEAVEN

John next reports on a war in heaven. "Now war arose in heaven, Michael[53] and his angels fighting against *the dragon*. And *the dragon and his angels* fought back, but he was *defeated*, and there was no longer any place for them in heaven. And *the great dragon was thrown down, that ancient serpent, who is called the devil and Satan, the deceiver of the whole world*—he was thrown down to the earth, and his angels were thrown down with him" (Rev. 12:7–9).

This defeat of Satan in heaven reflects Luke's narrative of the seventy-two returning to Jesus "with joy, saying, 'Lord, even the *demons* are subject to us in your name!' And he said to them, 'I saw *Satan* fall like lightning from heaven'" (Luke 10:17–18). "The defeat of Satan began with the first coming of Christ."[54]

The defeat of Satan in heaven also spells victory for the kingdom of God and great rejoicing in heaven. "And I heard a loud voice in heaven, saying, 'Now the salvation and the power and *the kingdom of our God and the authority of his Christ have come*, for the *accuser* of our brothers has been thrown down, who accuses them day and night before our God. And they *have conquered him by the blood of the Lamb* and by the word of their testimony,

---

52. See David Barrett and Todd M. Johnson, *World Christian Encyclopedia* (2d ed.; New York: Oxford University Press, 2001), 1:11.

53. "One of the chief princes" (Dan. 10:13). See Daniel 12:1: "At that time [of the end] shall arise Michael, the great prince who has charge of your people." See Jude 9: "The archangel Michael, contending with the devil, was disputing about the body of Moses."

54. Anthony Hoekema, *The Bible and the Future*, 227, referring to Revelation 12:7–9.

for they loved not their lives even unto death. Therefore, rejoice, O heavens and you who dwell in them! But woe to you, O *earth and sea*, for the *devil* has come down to you in great wrath, because he knows that his time is short!'" (Rev. 12:10–12).

WAR ON EARTH

With Satan and his angels thrown down to earth, the battlefield shifts from heaven to earth for a period of war described variously as three-and-a-half years, forty-two months, and 1,260 days.

> And when the *dragon* saw that he had been thrown down to the earth, he pursued the woman [Israel/the church] who had given birth to the male child [the Messiah Jesus]. But the woman was given the two wings of the great eagle so that she might fly from the *serpent* into the *wilderness*, to the place where she is to be *nourished for a time, and times, and half a time*.[55] The *serpent* poured *water like a river* out of his mouth after the woman, to sweep her away with a *flood* [chaos]. But the earth came to the help of the woman, and the earth opened its mouth and swallowed the *river* that the *dragon* had poured from his mouth. Then the *dragon* became furious with the woman and went off to make war on the rest of her offspring,[56] on those who keep the commandments of God and hold to the testimony of Jesus. And he stood on the sand of the *sea* [ready to call up his helper from the depths of chaos]. (Rev. 12:13–17)

---

55. 1 time + 2 times + ½ time = 3½ years = one half of a complete period of 7 times = 1,260 days (Rev. 12:6) of nourishment in the gospel age/the church age.

56. Persecution of individual Christians in the same period that the church as a whole is nourished in the wilderness.

BEASTS FROM THE SEA AND THE EARTH ASSIST SATAN

In his pursuit of God's people, Satan first calls up a beast from the depths of the sea. Daniel had portrayed evil world empires coming up from the sea. John follows suit in Revelation 13:

> And I saw a *beast*[57] rising out of the *sea* [chaos], with ten horns [a full number of kings, see 17:12] and seven heads [a complete number of emperors], with ten diadems on its horns and blasphemous names [such as "Lord," "Savior," "Son of God" claimed by Roman emperors] on its heads. And the *beast* that I saw was like a leopard; its feet were like a bear's, and its mouth was like a lion's mouth [a monstrous mutant]. And to it the *dragon* [Satan] gave his power and his throne and great authority. One of its heads seemed to have a mortal wound, but its mortal wound was healed, and the *whole earth* marveled as they *followed the beast*. And *they worshiped the dragon* [Satan], for he had given his authority to the beast, and *they worshiped the beast*, saying, "Who is like the *beast*, and who can fight against it?"
>
> And the *beast* was given a mouth uttering haughty and blasphemous words, and it was allowed to *exercise authority for forty-two months* [the three-and-a-half years, the 1,260 days of the gospel age]. It opened its mouth to utter *blasphemies against God*, blaspheming his name and his dwelling, that is, those who dwell in heaven. Also it was allowed to make *war on the saints and to conquer them* [chaos]." (Rev. 13:1–7)

---

57. The Roman Empire. See Revelation 17:3, 6–9: "I saw a woman sitting on a scarlet beast that was full of blasphemous names, and it had seven heads and ten horns. . . . And I saw the woman, drunk with the blood of the saints, the blood of the martyrs of Jesus. When I saw her, I marveled greatly. But the angel said to me, 'Why do you marvel? I will tell you the mystery of the woman, and of the beast with seven heads and ten horns that carries her. The beast that you saw was, and is not, and is about to rise from the *bottomless pit* and go to destruction. . . . This calls for a mind with wisdom: the seven heads are seven mountains on which the woman is seated." Rome was known as the city on seven hills.

Satan is also aided by a beast from the earth, later called "the false prophet."[58] John writes, "Then I saw *another beast* rising out of the earth.[59] It had two horns like a lamb and it *spoke like a dragon* [innocent as a lamb but an agent of Satan]. It *exercises all the authority of the first beast* in its presence, and *makes the earth and its inhabitants worship the first beast*, whose mortal wound was healed. It performs great signs,[60] even making fire come down from heaven to earth in front of people, and by the signs that it is allowed to work in the presence of the beast it *deceives those who dwell on earth*" (Rev. 13:11–14). These two assistants of Satan, the beast from the sea and the false prophet, will produce utter chaos on earth.

CHRIST CONQUERS THE BEAST AND FALSE PROPHET

In Revelation 19 John saw heaven, where Christ reigns in glory, opened and Christ, (presumably) coming down to earth, to make war on the evil nations, especially the beast and the false prophet who had deceived the nations. John writes:

> Then I saw *heaven opened*, and behold, *a white horse*! The one sitting on it is called Faithful and True, and *in righteousness he judges and makes war*. His eyes are like a flame of fire, and on his head are many diadems, and he has a name written that no one knows but himself. He is clothed in *a robe dipped in blood* [see Isa. 63:1–6], and the name by which he is called

---

58. "And I saw, coming out of the mouth of the *dragon* and out of the mouth of the *beast* and out of the mouth of *the false prophet*, three unclean spirits like frogs" (Rev. 16:13).

59. "The beast from the earth and the beast from the sea appear very much like Behemoth and Leviathan in Job, chs. 40, 41. . . . Since both of these beasts play such an important part in Jewish Apocalyptic writings, the author of the Book of Revelation would turn to them in attempting to paint the vivid picture of the coming of the last days." Wallace, "Leviathan and the Beast in Revelation," 67–68.

60. See Jesus's warning, "False christs and false prophets will arise and perform signs and wonders, to lead astray, if possible, the elect. But be on guard; I have told you all things beforehand" (Mark 13:22–23). See also Paul's warning in 2 Thessalonians 2:9–10: "The coming of the lawless one is by the activity of *Satan* with all power and *false signs and wonders*, and with all wicked deception for those who are perishing."

is *The Word of God* [John 1:1; 1 John 1:1]. And the *armies of heaven*,[61] arrayed in fine linen, white and pure, were following him on white horses. From his mouth comes a sharp sword[62] with which to strike down the nations, and he will *rule them with a rod of iron*.[63] He will tread the winepress of the fury of the wrath of God the Almighty. On his robe and on his thigh he has a name written, *King of kings and Lord of lords*.[64]

... And I saw *the beast and the kings of the earth* with their armies gathered to *make war* against *him who was sitting on the horse and against his army*. And the *beast* was captured, and with it the *false prophet* who in its presence had done the signs by which he deceived those who had received the mark of the beast and those who worshiped its image. These two were *thrown alive into the lake of fire* that burns with sulfur [hell; ultimate chaos]. And the rest were slain by *the sword that came from the mouth*[65] of him who was sitting on the horse, and all the birds were gorged with their flesh." (Rev. 19:11–16, 19–21)

The King of kings and the armies of heaven soundly defeat the beast and the false prophet who caused so much chaos on earth. That leaves Satan as the last instigator of chaos.

---

61. See Psalm 68:17: "The chariots of God are twice ten thousand, thousands upon thousands; the Lord is among them."

62. A symbol of judgment. See Isaiah 11:4 and Hebrews 4:12.

63. See Psalm 2:9 regarding the Lord's son: "You shall break them [the nations] with a rod of iron."

64. Compare Revelation 17:14: "They will make war on the Lamb, and the Lamb will conquer them, for he is *Lord of lords and King of kings*, and those with him are called and chosen and faithful." See also 1 Timothy 6:14–15: "Our Lord Jesus Christ. . . . he who is the blessed and only Sovereign, the King of kings and Lord of lords."

65. See Revelation 1:16: "In his right hand he held seven stars, from his mouth came a sharp two-edged sword."

Questions for Reflection

1. The book of Revelation is apocalyptic literature. What are some characteristics of apocalyptic literature?

2. Revelation 1 speaks of two realities: the seven churches undergoing the chaos of tribulation and the risen, glorified Christ being in the midst of his churches. Give some examples of the Christian church being persecuted today. Have you yourself suffered some form of persecution? How is the presence of Christ a comfort to persecuted Christians?

3. Revelation 2 speaks of the instigator of chaos, Satan, the Devil. How did Satan introduce chaos into God's good creation? How does Satan continue to promote chaos on earth?

4. Genesis 11:1–9 gives the account of the tower of Babel and the chaos of different languages. When was this chaos temporarily lifted? Where and when do you think this chaos of languages will be permanently lifted?

5. Track the sequence of events presented in the apocalyptic images of Revelation 12:1–6 with the historical events reported in the Gospels and Acts.

6. Revelation 12:6 speaks of "1,260 days," 12:14 of "a time, and times, and half a time," and 13:5 speaks of "forty-two months"—roughly the same time period. What is that time period? What two major things will happen in that time period?

7. According to Revelation 13:1–14, Satan is aided by two beasts. The first beast came "out of the sea" (v. 1). What does this tell you? The other beast "spoke like a dragon" (v. 11). What does this tell you? What evil things do they do?

8. Are these beasts active today? If so, how?

9. Revelation 19:11 speaks of a *white* horse. In the light of our chaos–cosmos discussion, why is the color white significant? Who is the rider on the white horse? What is the meaning of the name, "King of kings and Lord of lords"?

10. Who does the King of kings and his army capture? What will they do with them? Which evil being is left by himself?

Chaos–Cosmos in Revelation 20–22

SATAN BOUND FOR A THOUSAND YEARS

As the apocalyptic book of Daniel has many symbolic numbers, so the book of Revelation has many symbolic numbers, especially 7, used fifty-seven times in Revelation, and 10 and its multiples 100, 1,000, 12,000, and 144,000, which are used numerous times. Ten is the number of fullness. The thousand years is 10 x 10 x 10, the number of fullness—therefore a full period of world history.

John writes in Revelation 20, "Then I saw an angel coming down from heaven, holding in his hand the key to the bottomless pit (*abyssou*) and a great chain.[66] And he seized the *dragon, that ancient serpent, who is the devil and Satan*, and *bound him for a thousand years*, and threw him into the *pit*, and shut it and sealed it over him, so that he might *not deceive the nations any longer, until the thousand years were ended*. After that he must be released for *a little while*" (Rev. 20:1–3).

As we saw earlier, Christ bound Satan when, at the beginning of his ministry, he withstood Satan's temptations in the wilderness. This allowed Jesus and his disciples to cast out demons and undermine Satan's dominion. When "the seventy-two returned with joy, saying, 'Lord, even the *demons* are subject to us in your name!'" Jesus said, "I saw *Satan* fall like lightning from heaven" (Luke 10:17–18).[67] From Jesus's first coming to the present time, Satan is bound in the sense that he is limited in his ability to "deceive the nations." In fact, John uses the same Greek verb, *deō*, for the binding of Satan as Jesus used in his parable for binding the strong man: "But no one can enter a

---

66. "*Abyssos* is the Septuagint rendering of *tĕhôm*, the watery deep. However, by New Testament times, it had become a bottomless pit full of fire and smoke." Wallace, "Leviathan and the Beast in Revelation," 67.

67. See Jesus's words a few days before his crucifixion: "Now is the judgment of this world; now will the ruler of this world be *cast out*. And I, when I am lifted up from the earth, *will draw all people to myself*" (John 12:31–32). Jesus's crucifixion spells the defeat of Satan and Jesus's victory in drawing all people to himself.

strong man's house and plunder his goods, unless he first *binds* the strong man. Then indeed he may plunder his house" (Mark 3:27). Satan is bound during this age of preaching the gospel. Like a lion on a chain, Satan can still hurt but is limited in his ability to deceive the nations on a worldwide scale (see Rev. 20:8–9).[68] "The binding of Satan during the gospel age means that, first, he cannot prevent the spread of the gospel, and second, he cannot gather all the enemies of Christ together to attack the church."[69]

In contrast to *pre*millennialism (Christ will return *before* the millennium) and *post*millennialism (Christ will return *after* the millennium), we can call this position "*present*-millennialism,"[70] that is, Christ inaugurated the millennium with his first coming so that we live in the millennium at the present time. Jesus ascended into heaven and presently rules at the right hand of God the Father. As we confess with the Apostles' Creed, we believe in Jesus Christ who "rose again from the dead; he ascended into heaven, and is seated at the right hand of God the Father almighty; from there he shall come to judge the living and the dead."

John continues in Revelation 20:

> Then I saw thrones, and seated on them were those to whom the authority to judge was committed. Also I saw the *souls* of

---

68. Jesus said, "And this gospel of the kingdom will be proclaimed throughout the whole world as a testimony *to all nations*, and *then the end will come*" (Matt. 24:14). Paul wrote, "For the mystery of lawlessness is already at work. Only he who now *restrains it* will do so until he is out of the way. And then the lawless one will be revealed, whom the Lord Jesus will kill with the breath of his mouth and bring to nothing by the appearance of his coming" (2 Thess. 2:7–8).

69. Hoekema, *The Bible and the Future*, 228. Hoekema continues, "Because of the binding of Satan during this present age, the nations cannot conquer the church, but the church is conquering the nations" (229).

70. To label this position "*amillennialism*" (*no* millennium), as is common, is much too simplistic and negative for a belief that celebrates the millennium as Christ's dominion over Satan from his first coming to his second coming because he rules from heaven being seated at the right hand of God the Father. Although Hoekema continues to use the term "amillennialism," he calls it "not a very happy" term: "It suggests that amillennialists either do not believe in any millennium or that they simply ignore the first six verses of Revelation 20, which speak of a millennial reign. Neither of these two statements is correct." *The Bible and the Future*, 173.

those who had been beheaded for the testimony of Jesus and for the word of God [Christian martyrs], and those who had not worshiped the beast or its image and had not received its mark on their foreheads or their hands. They *came to life* and *reigned with Christ for a thousand years* [reigned with Christ in heaven[71]]. The rest of the dead did not come to life until the thousand years were ended. This is the *first resurrection* [from physical death to reigning with Christ in heaven]. Blessed and holy is the one who shares in the first resurrection! Over such the *second death* ["the lake of fire" (20:14), hell] has no power, but they will be priests of God and of Christ, and they will reign with him [in heaven] for a *thousand years* [until Christ's second coming]. (Rev. 20:4–6)

Satan Will Be Released, Defeated, and Thrown into Hell

Just prior to Jesus's second coming, Satan will be released for a little while to deceive the nations and make war on Christians. This is the great tribulation.[72] John continues in Revelation 20, "And when the thousand years are ended, *Satan* will be released from his prison and will come out to *deceive the nations* that are at the four corners of the earth, Gog and Magog,[73] to gather them for battle; their number is like the sand of the sea. And they marched up over the broad plain of the earth and *surrounded the camp of the saints and the beloved city*, but fire came down from heaven and consumed them, and the *devil*

---

71. "The reigning of the souls of deceased believers with Christ in heaven has had good standing in the church since the days of Augustine." Hoekema, *The Bible and the Future*, 183, with a reference to Augustine's *City of God*, xx, 9–10.

72. Jesus said, "For then there will be *great tribulation* ["great suffering," NRSV], such as has not been from the beginning of the world until now, no, and never will be. And if those days had not been cut short, no human being would be saved. But for the sake of the elect those days will be cut short" (Matt. 24:21–22).

73. Gog and Magog were enemies of Israel who formed a coalition of nations to destroy God's people. See Ezekiel 38–39.

who had deceived them was *thrown into the lake of fire and sulfur* [ultimate chaos] where the beast and the false prophet were, and they will be tormented day and night forever and ever" (Rev. 20:7–10). Ironically, the personifications of chaos—the beast from the sea, the false prophet from the earth, and now the Devil himself—will forever suffer in hell, the ultimate form of chaos.

CHRIST'S SECOND COMING, RESURRECTION OF THE DEAD, AND FINAL JUDGMENT

John continues in Revelation 20:

> Then I saw a great white throne and him [Christ] who was seated on it. From his presence earth and sky fled away, and no place was found for them. And I saw the *dead*, great and small, standing before the throne,[74] and books were opened. Then another book was opened, which is the book of life. And the dead were judged by what was written in the books, according to *what they had done*. And the *sea* gave up the *dead* who were in it, *Death and Hades* [Heb. *Sheol*] gave up the *dead* who were in them, and they were *judged*, each one of them, according to *what they had done*. Then *Death and Hades were thrown into the lake of fire*. This is the *second death*, the lake of fire. And if anyone's name was not found written in the book of life, he was thrown into the lake of fire. (Rev. 20:11–15)

Christ's second coming and the final judgment will mark the end of every form of chaos on earth: it will mark the end not only for those who supported chaos with their actions but also for death itself

---

74. The resurrection. See 1 Corinthians 15:22–23: "For as in Adam all die, so also in Christ shall all be made alive. But each in his own order: Christ the firstfruits, then at his coming those who belong to Christ." See also Philippians 3:20–21 and 1 Thessalonians 4:16.

and the realm of the dead (Hades, Sheol), which will be thrown into the lake of fire, the "outer darkness."

A New Heaven and a New Earth

John follows up this elimination from the earth of every form of chaos with a vision of a new cosmos. He writes in Revelation 21:1, "Then I saw *a new heaven and a new earth*,[75] for the first heaven and the first earth had passed away, and *the sea was no more*." The expression "*new* heaven and *new* earth" (not *neos* but *kainos*) means "not the emergence of a cosmos totally other than the present one, but the creation of a universe which, though it has been gloriously renewed, stands in continuity with the present one."[76] We shall note several items that will be renewed.

No More Sea

The first item John mentions about the new earth is that "the sea was no more." The sea—the primary symbol of chaos in the Bible—was no more.[77] No more chaos; no more dis-cosmos, but only perfect cosmos in God's new creation.

But the assertion that there will be no more evil sea does not mean that the new earth will have no seas. According to Genesis 1:10 God called the seas "good." There will be continuity between the seas of God's first creation and those of the new creation. In Revelation 10:6–7 the angel standing on the sea and on the land "swore by him who lives forever and ever, who created heaven and what is in it, the earth and what is in it, and *the sea and what is in it*." Here there are no

---

75. See Isaiah 65:17: "For behold, I create new heavens and a new earth, and the former things shall not be remembered or come into mind." See also Isaiah 66:22.

76. Hoekema, *The Bible and the Future*, 280.

77. "The turbulent waters, the sea, which had been in rebellion against the gods in Babylonian mythology, against Baal in Canaanite literature, and against Yahweh in the O.T., the sea was gone! This is a graphic symbol of the complete abolition of evil in the world." Wallace, "Leviathan and the Beast in Revelation," 68.

evil connotations for the sea. In fact, in Revelation 5:13 John "heard every creature in heaven and on earth and under the earth and *in the sea, and all that is in them*, saying, 'To him who sits on the throne and to the Lamb be blessing and honor and glory and might forever and ever!'" If every creature in the sea praises God and the Lamb, the sea and its creatures cannot be considered evil. There will be refreshing, nourishing waters on the new earth.[78]

God Dwelling with His People

The second renewed event is God dwelling with his people. In the beginning God dwelt with his people in Paradise (Gen. 3:8), "the garden of God" (Isa. 51:3; Ezek. 28:13). But with the fall into sin God withdrew his special presence from Paradise into heaven. At Babel "the LORD *came down* to see the city and the tower, which the children of man had built" (Gen. 11:5). The Lord was called "the God of heaven."[79]

Walton states, "In the aftermath of the fall, the greatest loss was not paradise but God's presence. The temple provided for a partial return of that presence."[80] Pentecost provided even more of a return of God's presence with the outpouring of the Holy Spirit. But there will be a complete return of God's presence in the new creation. John writes, "And I saw the holy city, new Jerusalem, coming down out of heaven from God, prepared as a bride adorned for her husband. And I heard a loud voice from the throne saying, 'Behold, *the*

---

78. See the discussion below (pp. 170–71) on the return of Paradise on earth, including "the river of the water of life."

79. For example, "The LORD, the God of heaven" (Gen. 24:7); "Turn again, O God of hosts! Look down from heaven, and see; have regard for this vine" (Ps. 80:14); "Give thanks to the God of heaven, for his steadfast love endures forever" (Ps. 136:26).

80. John H. Walton, *Ancient Near Eastern Thought and the Old Testament: Introducing the Conceptual World of the Hebrew Bible* (Grand Rapids, MI: Baker, 2006), 125. See Exodus 25:8: "And let them make me a sanctuary, that I may dwell in their midst." See also Isaiah 12:6: "Shout, and sing for joy, O inhabitant of Zion, for great in your midst is the Holy One of Israel," and Zechariah 2:10: "Sing and rejoice, O daughter of Zion, for behold, I come and I will dwell in your midst, declares the LORD."

dwelling place of God is with man. He will dwell with them, and they will be his people, and *God himself will be with them* as their God'" (Rev. 21:2–3).[81]

No More Death

The third renewed aspect of the new creation is that there will be no more death. As we just saw: "Death and Hades were thrown into the lake of fire" (Rev. 20:14)—finished. John continues in Revelation 21, "He [God] will wipe away every tear from their eyes, and *death shall be no more*" (Rev. 21:4).[82] Death shall be no more because Jesus died and rose again and has "the keys of Death and Hades."[83] In the new creation, the curse of death (Gen. 3:19) is lifted. Chaos is conquered.

No More Mourning, Crying, or Pain

With the lifting of the curse of death, its effects on loved ones is also lifted: no more mourning, crying, or pain. John writes, "Death shall be no more, *neither shall there be mourning, nor crying,*[84] *nor pain anymore,* for the former things [chaos] have passed away. And he who was seated on the throne said, 'Behold, I am making all things new'" (Rev. 21:4–5). The cosmos God intended in the beginning will be restored.

No Temple, Sun, Moon, or Night in the New Jerusalem

John continues by describing the holy city Jerusalem: "And he carried me away in the Spirit to a great, high mountain, and showed me the holy city Jerusalem coming down out of heaven from God" (Rev. 21:10).

81. See Leviticus 26:11–12: "I will make my dwelling among you. . . . And I will walk among you and will be your God, and you shall be my people." See also Ezekiel 37:27: "My dwelling place shall be with them, and I will be their God, and they shall be my people."

82. See Isaiah 25:8: "He [the LORD of hosts] will swallow up death forever; and the Lord GOD will wipe away tears from all faces."

83. Jesus said, "Fear not, I am the first and the last, and the living one. I died, and behold I am alive forevermore, and I have the keys of Death and Hades" (Rev. 1:17–18).

84. See Revelation 7:17: "God will wipe away every tear from their eyes."

These are the renewed things John saw in the new Jerusalem: "And I saw *no temple* in the city, *for its temple is the Lord God the Almighty and the Lamb*" (Rev. 21:22). As we saw above, the temple provided only a partial return of God's presence. Since God himself will dwell with his people in the new Jerusalem (Rev. 21:3), the temple will no longer be necessary.

John continues, "And the city has *no need of sun or moon to shine on it, for the glory of God gives it light,*[85] *and its lamp is the Lamb.* By its *light* [cosmos] will the *nations* walk, and the kings of the earth will bring their glory into it, and its gates will never be shut by day—and there will be *no night* [no chaos] there" (Rev. 21:23–25). In the new Jerusalem there will be no more night, no more darkness, no more chaos, but all will be light—cosmos.

THE RETURN OF PARADISE ON EARTH

John continues in Revelation 22:

> Then the angel showed me the *river of the water of life,*[86] bright as crystal, flowing from the throne of God and of the Lamb through the middle of the street of the city; also, on either side of the *river, the tree of life* [Gen. 2:9] with its twelve kinds of fruit, yielding its fruit each month. The leaves of the tree were for the healing of the nations.[87] *No longer* will there be

---

85. Creation's lights take a back seat to the light of God and the Lamb. See Isaiah 60:19–20: "The sun shall be no more your light by day, nor for brightness shall the moon give you light; but the LORD will be your everlasting light, and your God will be your glory. Your sun shall no more go down, nor your moon withdraw itself; for the LORD will be your everlasting light, and your days of mourning shall be ended."

86. See Genesis 2:10. See also Joel 3:18: "And in that day . . . a fountain shall come forth from the house of the LORD and water the Valley of Shittim"; Ezekiel 47:1: "The water was flowing down from below the south end of the threshold of the temple"; and Zechariah 14:8 "On that day living waters shall flow out from Jerusalem. . . . It shall continue in summer as in winter."

87. See Ezekiel 47:12: "And on the banks, on both sides of the river, there will grow all kinds of trees for food. Their leaves will not wither, nor their fruit fail, but they will bear fresh fruit every month, because the water for them flows from the sanctuary. Their fruit will be for food, and their leaves for healing."

anything accursed [the curse, Gen. 3:17, will be lifted], but the throne of God and of the Lamb will be in it, and his servants will worship him. They will *see his face*,[88] and his name will be on their foreheads. And *night* [darkness, chaos] *will be no more*. They will need no light of lamp or sun, for the Lord God will be their *light*, and they will reign forever and ever. (Rev. 22:1–5)

In the beginning of the book of Revelation the risen Lord Jesus promised his followers, "To the one who conquers I will grant to *eat of the tree of life*, which is in the *paradise* of God" (Rev. 2:7). In concluding the book, the Lord Jesus repeated, "Blessed are those who wash their robes, so that they may have *the right to the tree of life*"—adding, "and that they may *enter the city* [the holy city, the new Jerusalem] by the gates" (Rev. 22:14). Paradise, the garden, with its life-giving waters and the tree of life as well as the holy city will return in the new creation.

———

We have now come full circle from the cosmos of Paradise in Genesis 1 to the cosmos of Paradise in Revelation 22. Chaos will be completely overcome: no more evil sea (21:1), no more death, no more mourning, crying, or pain (21:4–5), no more night/darkness (21:25; 22:5), no more anything accursed (22:3). God's curse on this fallen creation will be lifted, and God will restore his creation to the orderly, harmonious cosmos he intended it to be from the beginning. What a marvelous vision of the future!

---

88. Note the contrast between Exodus 33:20: "You cannot see my face, for man shall not see me and live," and Jesus's words in Matthew 5:8: "Blessed are the pure in heart, for they shall see God." We see the face of God in Jesus. Jesus said, "Whoever has seen me has seen the Father" (John 14:9). See 1 John 3:2: "We know that when he appears we shall be like him, because we shall see him as he is."

Questions for Reflection

1. Revelation 20:2 says that the angel "seized the dragon, that ancient serpent, who is the devil and Satan, and bound him for *a thousand years*." How should the thousand years be understood, literally as a one-thousand year period or figuratively as a full period of world history? Give reasons for your answer.

2. Revelation 20:7–10 speaks of Satan's final attempt to snuff out the church worldwide. Are you concerned for yourself or your children and grandchildren about that violent future? Who defeats Satan in this final battle and how?

3. Revelation 20:11–15 speaks of the final judgment. Do you fear the final judgment? Why or why not?

4. Revelation 20:12 says, "And the dead were judged by what was written in the books, *according to what they had done*" (see Rev. 22:12). How can you harmonize "according to what they had done" with *sola gratia*, salvation by grace alone, such as Paul teaches in Ephesians 2:8–10: "For by grace you have been saved through faith. And this is not your own doing; it is the gift of God, *not a result of works*, so that no one may boast. For we are his workmanship, created in Christ Jesus for good works, which God prepared beforehand, that we should walk in them."

5. In light of our study, what is the meaning of Revelation 20:14: "Then Death and Hades were thrown into the lake of fire"?

6. In Revelation 21:1 John writes, "Then I saw a new heaven and a new earth, for the first heaven and the first earth had passed away, and *the sea was no more*." Will there be seas on the new earth? Argue your case biblically.

7. List the forms of orderly cosmos that will characterize the new heaven and new earth according to Revelation 21:1–5.

8. Compare the picture of the original Paradise (Gen. 2:8–17) with the picture of Revelation 22:1–5. Which elements occur in both pictures? Which elements are missing in the final picture? What do you think of 22:5: "And *night* will be no more"? What has Revelation 22:1–5 added to the picture of Genesis 2:8–17?

9. Why do you think Jesus promised not only a new Paradise but also a new Jerusalem? (See Rev. 21:1–22:5.)

10. In Revelation 22 Jesus says three times, "I am coming soon" (vv. 7, 12, 20). Do you think the "soon" seems to be taking a long time? See 2 Peter 3:8–13. Could "soon" also have the sense of "unexpectedly"? See Mark 13:32–37 and 1 Thessalonians 5:1–11.

11. Are you prepared for Jesus's coming? List what it takes to be ready for Jesus's sudden coming according to:

    Jesus (Matt. 25:13–46)
    Paul (Acts 16:30–34)
    James (James 2:14–17)
    Peter (2 Pet. 3:10–14)

Preaching or Teaching a Series on the Chaos–Cosmos Theme

Preaching or teaching a series of sermons or lessons on the chaos–cosmos theme will make the hearers more aware of the unity of the Scriptures and the centrality of Christ in the Scriptures. It will also shape their world and life views, deepening their understanding of the original creation and the coming new creation. They will become more aware of the goodness and harmony of God's creation (cosmos) and the disastrous consequences of the fall into sin, which is ever more evident in the various forms of chaos we see all around us. But they will also be comforted and encouraged when they become more aware of God's sovereignty over chaos, God's grace for his fallen creatures, God's faithfulness to his creation, and God's intent to restore his creation to the orderly cosmos he intended it to be in the beginning.

Since the chaos–cosmos theme runs from Genesis 1 to Revelation 22, from the first creation to the new creation, there are many ways to preach a series of Christocentric sermons on this theme. One can select a preaching text anywhere along the chaos–cosmos trail and trace it forward to Jesus's first and/or second coming. However, tracing a longitudinal theme in detail in a sermon is rather cumbersome; it may result in sermons that are alike in their moves to Christ. Or, what's worse, it may stall sermons so that they crash instead of delivering the good news.

A Series of Fourteen Sermons or Lessons

One effective way to preach on the whole chaos–cosmos theme is to prepare a series of fourteen sermons or lessons. The effect of this series can be much enhanced if each sermon or lesson is followed by small group discussions on Sunday evening or during the following week. For that reason, I have provided reading assignments for small groups in the appendix. I suggest the following key passages and sermon themes:

1. Genesis 1:1–2:3. In the beginning God, having created the good building blocks of chaos, uses his powerful word to structure chaos into a harmonious cosmos (see pp. 27–33).

2. Genesis 3. God banishes sinners from the garden of Eden to live on the cursed ground east of Eden with a view to eventually restore an orderly cosmos on earth (see pp. 33–37).

3. Exodus 14. God saves Israel from the chaotic sea (see pp. 47–48).[1]

4. Job 1:6–2:10. God allows Satan (the instigator of chaos) to test the righteous Job (see pp. 58–59).

5. Psalm 2. In his battle with the kings of the earth (chaos), the Lord will gain worldwide victory (cosmos) through his anointed King (see pp. 77–78).[2]

---

1. One could substitute a sermon on Exodus 15:1–21, the Songs of Moses and Miriam (see pp. 48–49).

2. See my *Preaching Christ from Psalms*, 214–39. One could substitute a sermon on Psalm 104 (see *Preaching Christ from Psalms*, 469–501, or Psalm 46: "God is our refuge and strength, a very present help [cosmos] in trouble [chaos]."

6. Isaiah 11:1–9. Through a new Davidic King the Lord will restore Paradise (orderly cosmos) on earth (see pp. 89–91).[3]

7. Ezekiel 47:1–12. The Lord will restore Paradise (cosmos) in the Promised Land (see pp. 103–104).[4]

8. Zechariah 3:1–10. Through his servant, the branch, the Lord will remove the wickedness (chaos) of Israel in a single day (see pp. 113–114).[5]

9. Daniel 12:1–4. After a time of severe trouble (chaos), God will deliver his people by raising them from the dead and giving them everlasting life (cosmos) (see p. 118).[6]

10. Mark 15:33–16:8. In the darkness (chaos), Jesus, forsaken (chaos) by God, suffers the chaos of death, but miraculously rises from death and lives forevermore (cosmos) (see pp. 131–32).

11. Acts 2:1–47. Jesus sends the Holy Spirit to turn the chaos of different languages (Babel) into an orderly cosmos of understanding and unity in the church (see pp. 135–36).

12. Romans 8:35–39. In the midst of suffering (chaos), we are more than conquerors (cosmos) through the love of God in Christ Jesus (see p. 143).[7]

13. Revelation 1:9–20. The risen Christ in the midst of the churches has the keys of death and Hades (chaos) (see pp. 151–52).[8]

---

3. One could substitute a sermon on Isaiah 65:17–25 (see pp. 92–93).

4. One could substitute a sermon on Jeremiah 51:1–58 (see pp. 97–100).

5. One could substitute a sermon on Joel 2:1–27 (see pp. 109–110).

6. See my *Preaching Christ from Daniel*, 387–91.

7. One could substitute a sermon on Ephesians 6:10–20 (see pp. 141–42).

8. One could substitute a sermon on Revelation 12:1–17 (pp. 154–57) or 19:11–21 (pp. 159–60).

14. Revelation 22:1–21. Jesus will come soon to restore Paradise (cosmos) on earth (see pp. 170–71).[9]

A Series of Seven Christocentric Sermons or Lessons[10]

Another effective way to preach on the chaos–cosmos theme is to prepare a series of seven sermons (or teach a series of seven lessons) on seven early, foundational preaching texts along the chaos–cosmos trail: Genesis 1:1–2:3; 2:4–25; 3:1–24; 6:9–8:22; 11:1–9; 11:27–12:9; and Exodus 14. Below I will suggest the sermon themes and different ways of moving forward from the Old Testament text to Christ in the New Testament. For preaching Christ, we can for each text select the most solid of seven roads to Christ or a combination thereof. There are seven possible, sometimes overlapping, ways to Christ:[11]

1. The way of redemptive-historical progression concentrates on God's redemptive act(s) proclaimed in a passage and its relation to God's dynamic redemptive history as it progresses steadily through the Old Testament until it comes to a climax in God's redemptive acts in Jesus's first and/or second coming.

2. The way of promise-fulfillment moves from God's promise of a coming Messiah to its fulfillment with Jesus's first or second coming.

3. The way of typology moves from an Old Testament type prefiguring Jesus to the antitype, Jesus himself. Typology is marked by analogy between the type and Jesus as well as escalation from the type to Jesus.

---

9. One could substitute a sermon on Revelation 21:1–27 (pp. 167–70).

10. Another option would be to start with a few of the seven foundational passages treated below and follow up with any of the Bible books treated above, for example, Job, Isaiah, Mark, John, or Revelation.

11. For a detailed explanation of these seven ways and their source in the New Testament, see my *Preaching Christ from the Old Testament: A Contemporary Hermeneutical Method* (Grand Rapids, MI: Eerdmans, 1999), 203–77.

4. The way of analogy notes the similarity between the teaching or goal of the author and the teaching or goal of Jesus. Since the church is the new Israel, one can find analogies between what God did for Israel and what God through Christ does for the church as well as analogies between what God required of Israel and what God through Christ requires of the church.

5. The way of longitudinal themes traces the theme (or subtheme) of the text through the Old Testament to Jesus Christ in the New Testament.

6. The way of New Testament references usually supports the other six ways to Christ by quoting New Testament verses that cite or allude to the Old Testament preaching text and link it to Christ.

7. The way of contrast moves to Christ by noting the contrast between the message of the Old Testament text and that of the New Testament—a contrast that exists because Christ has come or because Christ teaches the opposite.

———

A SERMON OR LESSON ON GENESIS 1:1–2:3

"From Chaos to Cosmos"

The sermon or lesson could begin with an explanation of Genesis 1:2 that God in the beginning created chaos—not the evil we usually associate with chaos, but a chaos that God declared to be good. This good chaos was the material that God would subsequently structure into an orderly cosmos. The sermon could highlight the seven words used in Genesis 1 for chaos, which will be used later in Scripture, either individually or in combination, to denote chaos: "without form," "void," "darkness," "the deep," "the waters" (1:2), "seas" (v. 10), and "sea creatures / monsters" (v. 21).

Next one can highlight how God with his powerful word (ten times "God said") created the cosmos and declared a perfect seven times that it was "good"—the seventh time, "very good." Even the seas and sea monsters God declared to be "good" (Gen. 1:10, 21). God created this world perfectly good. The sermon theme, then, could be formulated as follows: *In the beginning God, having created the good building blocks of chaos, used his powerful word to structure chaos into a harmonious cosmos.*

The dominant goal of preaching this passage and the other six in this series is to teach the chaos–cosmos theme as it develops from the beginning of Scripture to its end. But we should not lose sight of other goals, such as to comfort, to give hope, and to encourage, which will lead to more relevant applications.[12]

A good move to Christ in the New Testament would be redemptive-historical progression supported by New Testament references. In contrast to tracing the biblical-theological theme, which could become tedious, the advantage of redemptive-historical progression is that one can leap across centuries to the New Testament. So after explaining Genesis 1:1–2:3 with its emphasis on "God said," one can use John 1:1–5, 14 to show that God's Word, through whom all things were made, was Jesus Christ: "In the beginning was the word. . . ." It would also be good to add Colossians 1:15–17, which makes the point that the whole cosmos hangs together in Christ: "He [Christ] is the image of the invisible God, the firstborn of all creation. For *by him all things were created*, in heaven and on earth, visible and invisible, whether thrones or dominions or rulers or authorities—*all*

12. For other goals than simply "to teach" and more details and suggestions for preaching these passages from Genesis, see my *Preaching Christ from Genesis*.

things were created through him and for him. And he is before all things, and *in him all things hold together.*"

A SERMON OR LESSON ON GENESIS 2:4–25

"The Garden of Eden: Cosmos"

In this text the narrator further explains how God made everything good for human beings. God himself fashioned the man from the dust of the ground and, in a very personal touch, breathed into his nostrils the breath of life. God placed him in a safe garden where God had provided plenty of food and meaningful work.[13] But then God discovered something "not good" in Paradise. The Lord said, "It is not good that the man should be alone; I will make him a helper fit for him" (Gen. 2:18). And God made a perfect partner for the man and brought her to him. The man was so excited, he broke into poetry:

> This at last is bone of my bones
> > and flesh of my flesh;
> she shall be called Woman (*'išāh*),
> > because she was taken out of Man (*'îš*). (Gen. 2:23)

The parallelism shows how closely the two were related: the same bones, the same flesh, but the opposite sex. They complemented each other perfectly.

The passage overflows with God's goodness for Adam and Eve—a picture of true cosmos. They could eat from every tree in the garden, including the tree of life. Even the single prohibition not to eat of "the tree of the knowledge of good and evil" was good because God treated human beings as moral agents who could willingly

---

13. "The LORD God took the man and put him in the garden of Eden to work it and keep it" (Gen. 2:15).

choose to obey God. Because of the safety, harmony, and goodness in the garden of Eden, we can formulate the sermon theme as follows: *God demonstrates his goodness to humankind by personally fashioning them as his special creatures, breathing into them the breath of life, in order to give them a meaningful task in a safe garden.*

A good way to move to Christ in the New Testament is a combination of contrast, promise-fulfillment, and New Testament references. Paul writes in Romans 8 about sufferings: tribulation, distress, persecution, famine, nakedness, danger, and sword (Rom. 8:35)—all forms of chaos. He writes, "We know that the whole creation has been *groaning* together in the pains of childbirth until now. And not only the creation, but *we ourselves*, who have the firstfruits of the Spirit, *groan inwardly* as we wait eagerly for adoption as sons, the redemption of our bodies" (Rom. 8:22–23). What a contrast with the cosmos of Paradise!

Today we not only experience some of Paul's sufferings but also new forms of chaos: terrorist threats, mass murders, suicide bombers, millions of refugees looking for a safe home, global warming. Israel also experienced sufferings when it was forcibly removed from the Promised Land ("well-watered everywhere like the garden of the Lord," Gen. 13:10) and enslaved in a foreign land. Their lives had become chaos instead of cosmos. But even while Israel was suffering through chaos, the Lord comforted them by promising that he would one day restore Paradise on earth. In Isaiah 51:3 the Lord promised:

> For the Lord comforts Zion;
>> he comforts all her waste places
> and makes her wilderness like *Eden*,
>> her desert like *the garden of the Lord* [cosmos];
> joy and gladness will be found in her,
>> thanksgiving and the voice of song.

In Isaiah 65 the Lord promised even more:

> For behold, I create new heavens
>> and a new earth. . . .
> But be glad and rejoice forever
>> in that which I create;
> for behold, I create Jerusalem to be a joy,
>> and her people to be a gladness.
> I will rejoice in Jerusalem
>> and be glad in my people;
> no more shall be heard in it the sound of weeping
>> and the cry of distress [no chaos]. . . .
> They shall build houses and inhabit them;
>> they shall plant vineyards and eat their fruit. . . .
> The wolf and the lamb shall graze together;
>> the lion shall eat straw like the ox [cosmos]. . . .
> They shall not hurt or destroy [no chaos]
>> in all my holy mountain,
>>>>> says the LORD. (vv. 17–19, 21, 25)

On the cross Jesus could say to the criminal next to him: "Truly, I say to you, today you will be with me in *Paradise*" (Luke 23:43). In fact, the risen Christ promised the churches, "To the one who conquers I will grant to eat of the *tree of life, which is in the paradise of God*" (Rev. 2:7). The last chapter in the Bible relates that John saw Paradise restored: he saw "the river of the water of life, bright as crystal, flowing from the throne of God and of the Lamb . . . ; also, on either side of the river, the *tree of life* with its twelve kinds of fruit, yielding its fruit each month. The leaves of the tree were for the *healing of the nations* [cosmos]" (Rev. 22:1–2). What a wonderful future we anticipate: the return of Paradise on earth—truly orderly cosmos!

A Sermon or Lesson on Genesis 3

"East of Eden: Chaos with Some Order"

This sermon should highlight the tragedy of the fall into sin. Although there was still some order because of God's faithfulness, cosmos gave way to partial chaos due to the fall. We see that chaos all around us today: senseless killings in our inner cities, nations using weapons of mass destruction, terrorist organizations, pollution and global warming. How did God's good creation get so chaotic?

In the first verse of Genesis 3 the narrator points to the main culprit: "Now *the serpent* was more crafty than any other beast of the field that the Lord God had made." There is something special about the serpent. In the Old Testament the serpent functions as a personification of chaos. In the book of Revelation John will later identify "the serpent" as "that ancient serpent, who is called the devil and Satan" (Rev. 12:9).

The serpent is up to no good. He wishes to spread chaos in this world. He tempts the woman to disobey God's command. God had commanded, "of the tree of the knowledge of good and evil you shall not eat, for in the day that you eat of it *you shall surely die*" (Gen. 2:17). The serpent bluntly contradicts God's word by saying: "'*You will not surely die*. For God knows that when you eat of it *your eyes will be opened*, and *you will be like God*, knowing good and evil.' So when the woman saw that the tree was good for food, and that it was a delight to the eyes, and that the tree was to be *desired to make one wise*, she took of its fruit and ate, and she also gave some to her husband who was with her, and he ate. *Then the eyes of both were opened*, and they knew that they were *naked*. And they sewed fig leaves together and made themselves loincloths" (Gen. 3:4–7). The result of their disobedience was not wisdom but an immediate loss of innocent harmony between them, followed by blaming others for their sin (vv. 12–13).

God punished their rebellion by introducing *enmity* between the serpent and the woman and their offspring, pain in childbearing, pain in gathering food from a cursed ground, and finally death. God drove them out of the cosmos of Eden into the chaos of living east of Eden on the cursed ground. With the fall into sin, chaos became evil.

But Genesis 3:15 holds out the promise of a reversal of God's curse:

> I will put enmity between you and the woman,
>> and between your offspring and her offspring;
> he shall bruise *your head* [a fatal wound],
>> and you shall bruise *his heel* [a nonlethal wound].

The sermon theme can be formulated as follows: *God banishes sinners from the garden of Eden to live on the cursed ground east of Eden with a view to eventually restore an orderly cosmos on earth.*

A good way to move to Christ in the New Testament is promise-fulfillment[14] combined with antithetic typology[15] and New Testament references. Genesis 3:15 contains the promise of victory for the offspring (seed) of the woman. Unlike the first Adam, Jesus, the second Adam, rejected Satan's clever temptations to abandon his road of suffering by gaining all the kingdoms of the world just by worshiping Satan (Matt. 4:1–11). Jesus received a serious wound when he died on the cross, but he rose again the victor over death and hell. Satan will receive a fatal wound when the victorious Christ at his second coming casts him into the lake of fire.[16] This elimination of the instigator of chaos will enable Jesus to restore cosmos on earth.

Describing the new earth, John writes, "No longer will there be

---

14. The church fathers called Genesis 3:15 *protevangelium*, the first gospel.

15. See my *Preaching Christ from Genesis*, 69.

16. See Revelation 20:10: "And the devil who had deceived them was thrown into the lake of fire and sulfur where the beast and the false prophet were, and they will be tormented day and night forever and ever."

anything accursed [chaos], but the throne of God and of the Lamb will be in it, and his servants will worship him. They will see his face, and his name will be on their foreheads. And night [chaos] will be no more. They will need no light of lamp or sun, for the Lord God will be their light, and they will reign forever and ever" (Rev. 22:3–5). Even when we suffer from chaos today, we can look forward to the day when Jesus will eliminate all accursed chaos, and we can joyfully worship God and the Lamb in a harmonious cosmos.

A Sermon or Lesson on Genesis 6:9–8:22

"The Flood: Chaos to Restore Cosmos"

One of the difficulties in preaching the flood narrative is its length, from Genesis 6:9–9:17. Although we can make our task more manageable by leaving chapter 9 for another sermon, even so the preaching text covers almost three chapters. Before the sermon, one could read only Genesis 6:9–22, while including selected verses from chapters 7 and 8 in the sermon itself.

The account of Noah and his descendants (the third *tôlĕdōt* of ten in Genesis) begins with a significant description of Noah: "These are the generations [*tôlĕdōt*] of Noah. Noah was a *righteous* man, *blameless* in his generation.[17] Noah *walked with God*" (Gen. 6:9). Noah was the exception, for the narrator continues: "Now the earth was *corrupt* in God's sight, and the earth was filled with *violence*" (6:11). This violence, this form of chaos, threatened to destroy God's creation. So God decided to return the earth to its original state of chaos with waters covering the entire earth (1:2) and beginning his creation anew.[18]

The flood narrative is about *God's judgment* of corruption and

---

17. "Blameless" is not sinless, but walking with integrity. See Psalm 101:2: "I will ponder the way that is *blameless*. . . . I will walk with *integrity* of heart within my house." See also Psalm 15:2–5.

18. For many similarities between the flood narrative and the creation narrative of Genesis 1, see my *Preaching Christ from Genesis*, 102, 115.

violence on the earth. God said to Noah, "I have determined to make *an end of all flesh*, for the earth is filled with violence through them. Behold, I will *destroy them* with the earth" (Gen. 6:13). But, amazingly, this narrative is also about God's grace, for God tells Noah to make an *ark* to save his family and the animals with him from the destructive waters (Gen. 6:13–22). In fact, the turn in the narrative occurs in chapter 8:1: "But God *remembered* Noah and all the beasts and all the livestock that were with him in the ark.[19] And God made a wind blow over the earth, and the waters subsided." Judgment and grace. We can, therefore, formulate the theme of this narrative as follows: *Even as God punished the world with a flood for its corruption and violence, in his grace God continues his kingdom on earth by making a new start with Noah, his family, and the animals in the ark.*

A good move to Christ in the New Testament is the road of typology, supported by New Testament references. The righteous Noah was a new Adam with whom God would make a new start. Noah "walked with God"; he obeyed God by faith, not by sight; he obeyed God without questioning by building an ark when there was not a cloud in the sky.[20] With Noah and all creatures in the ark, God would make a new start in developing this world as his kingdom.

The righteous Noah prefigures Jesus Christ. Jesus, "the son of Noah . . . the son of Adam,"[21] also "walked with God." He obeyed his Father without questioning, even when his Father's will would lead to his death on a cross. Jesus is the second Adam with whom God would make a new start in establishing his kingdom on earth.

19. God "remembers" in order to save. See Genesis 19:29; 30:22.
20. See Hebrews 11:7: "By faith Noah, being warned by God concerning events *as yet unseen*, in reverent fear constructed an ark for the saving of his household." See also Genesis 6:22 and 7:5: "Noah did this; he did all that God commanded him . . . And Noah did all that the LORD had commanded him."
21. See Luke 3:36–38. In contrast to Matthew, Luke, writing to Gentiles, traces Jesus's genealogy back to Adam (3:23–38) to emphasize that Jesus came for the whole human race.

But "something greater than [Noah] is here."[22] Jesus was not just "the son of Adam" but *God's* only Son. Jesus was not just *righteous* like Noah but *sinless*. Jesus, not Noah, battled the prince of chaos to establish God's cosmos on earth. Jesus said, "If it is by the Spirit of God that I cast out demons, then the kingdom of God has come upon you" (Matt. 12:28). Jesus, not Noah, is "the Lamb of God, who takes away the sin of the world!" (John 1:29).[23] Jesus, not Noah, paid for our sins by his atoning death on the cross. Jesus, not Noah, rose from the dead, conquering the chaos of death for us. When Jesus comes again, he will establish the worldwide kingdom of God in perfection. As Peter wrote, "According to his promise we are waiting for new heavens and a new earth in which *righteousness* dwells" (2 Pet. 3:13).

A Sermon or Lesson on Genesis 11:1–9

"Babel: The Chaos of Languages to Protect Cosmos"

Genesis 11 begins: "Now the whole earth had *one language and the same words.*" This single language enabled people to work well together. Unfortunately, it also enabled them to defy God's command to fill the earth. Genesis 1:28 tells us about God's plan for the human race: "And God blessed them. And God said to them, 'Be fruitful and multiply and *fill the earth and subdue it*, and *have dominion. . . .*'" God's intent was that human beings would fill the earth and, as image bearers of God, have dominion to the ends of the earth. God wanted the whole earth to mirror the cosmos of his kingdom.

After the flood, God repeated this mandate: "And God blessed Noah and his sons and said to them, 'Be fruitful and multiply and

---

22. See Matthew 12:41–42: "Something greater than Jonah is here. . . . Something greater than Solomon is here."

23. See 1 John 2:2: "He is the propitiation for our sins, and not for ours only but also for the sins of the whole world."

fill the earth'" (Gen. 9:1). But at Babel, people defied God's creation mandate. To cope with the chaos east of Eden, they said, "Come, let us build ourselves a city and a tower with its top in the heavens,[24] and let us make a name for ourselves, *lest we be dispersed over the face of the whole earth*" (Gen. 11:4). They sought salvation in their unity and ingenuity. The people, lusting for power, independence, and autonomy, would build a city and a tower with its top in the heavens so that they could stay together and always find their way back home. The proud people of Babel were set on building a local, secular city. But this would undermine God's plan of spreading his kingdom to the ends of the earth.

From highest heaven, however, "the LORD came down to see the city and the tower, which the children of man had built. And the LORD said, 'Behold, they are one people, and they have all one language, and this is only the beginning of what they will do. And nothing that they propose to do will now be impossible for them. Come, let us go down and there confuse their language, so that they may not understand one another's speech.' So the LORD *dispersed them from there over the face of all the earth*, and they left off building the city" (Gen. 11:5–8).

In the conclusion the narrator repeats one more time, "Therefore its name was called Babel, because there the LORD confused the language of all the earth. And from there the LORD dispersed them over the face of all the earth" (Gen. 11:9). We can formulate the theme of this passage as follows: *In the interest of spreading his kingdom over the face of all the earth, the Lord confused the common human language into the chaos of many languages.*

A good move to Christ in the New Testament would be a combination

---

24. See Isaiah 14:13–14: "You said in your heart, 'I will ascend to heaven; above the stars of God I will set my throne on high . . . ; I will ascend above the heights of the clouds; I will make myself *like the Most High*.'"

of redemptive-historical progression and promise-fulfillment supported by New Testament references. The Lord interrupted the rise of a local, monolithic secular city by confusing the common human language. This forced people to spread around the globe and form different nations. This, in turn, allowed God to make a new start with one family, Abram's, and one nation, Israel. In the fullness of time Jesus was born of the nation of Israel.

When Jesus had fulfilled his mission on earth, he ascended into heaven. But he promised, "You will receive power when the Holy Spirit has come upon you, and you will be my witnesses in Jerusalem and in all Judea and Samaria, and *to the end of the earth*" (Acts 1:8). The creation mandate to spread God's kingdom to the end of the earth would be fulfilled by the Holy Spirit through the church.

On the day of Pentecost Jesus sent the promised Spirit, with amazing results. "And they were all filled with *the Holy Spirit* and began to speak in *other tongues* as the Spirit gave them utterance." People "from every nation under heaven" were bewildered "because *each one was hearing them speak in his own language* . . . the mighty works of God" (Acts 2:4–6, 11).

Pentecost reversed for the early church the chaos of Babel. And the result was orderly cosmos: people understanding each other and an amazing sense of unity in the church, even to sharing their possessions: "All who believed were together and had *all things in common. And they were selling their possessions and belongings and distributing the proceeds to all, as any had need.* And day by day, attending the temple together and breaking bread in their homes, they received their food with glad and generous hearts, praising God and having favor with all the people. And the Lord added to their number day by day *those who were being saved*" (Acts 2:44–47). The church experienced temporarily a foretaste of Paradise on earth, but this was only a small beginning.

Zephaniah had prophesied that one day God will for all time reverse the chaos of Babel: "For at that time *I will change the speech of the peoples to a pure speech*, that *all of them* may call upon the name of the LORD and *serve him with one accord*" (Zeph. 3:9). On Patmos, John saw the fulfillment of this prophecy: "After this I looked, and behold, a great multitude that no one could number, *from every nation, from all tribes and peoples and languages*, standing before the throne and before the Lamb, clothed in white robes, with palm branches in their hands, and crying out with a loud voice, '*Salvation* belongs to our God who sits on the throne, and to the Lamb!'" (Rev. 7:9–10). Not human ingenuity but God and Jesus accomplish salvation. The common language in heaven is a foretaste of the pure cosmos on the new earth when a united people of God will use a common language to honor God the Father and his Son Jesus for their salvation. Once again we see that the sovereign God can use chaos to promote his ultimate intent to create orderly cosmos.

A SERMON OR LESSON ON GENESIS 11:27–12:9

"God Gives the Land of the Cursed Canaanites to Obedient Abram"

The chaos of many languages resulted in seventy (7 x 10) nations, "each with his own language" (Gen. 10:5).[25] The narrator begins with the genealogy of Terah from the line of Shem, the seed of the woman:[26] "Now these are the generations of Terah. Terah fathered Abram, Nahor, and Haran; and Haran fathered Lot" (Gen. 11:27). They lived in Ur of the Chaldeans.

---

25. For reasons why the narrator may have reversed Genesis 10, the table of nations, and Genesis 11:1–9, see my *Preaching Christ from Genesis*, 120.

26. Noah said, "'Cursed be Canaan; a servant of servants shall he be to his brothers.' He also said, 'Blessed be the LORD, the God of Shem; and let Canaan be his servant'" (Gen. 9:25–26).

"Now the LORD said to Abram, 'Go from your country and your kindred and your father's house to the land that I will show you'" (Gen. 12:1). God wanted to separate Abram from his country (Chaldea, Babylonia), his kindred (distant relatives), and even from his father's house (his immediate family). In short, God wanted to separate Abram from the nations in order to make a new start with him and his family in the land God would show him. That land turned out to be Canaan, which was watered "like the garden of the LORD" (Gen. 13:10). Canaan would be another Paradise, a beachhead for the cosmos of the kingdom of God on earth.

Since he was the seed of the woman, Abram was to carry the banner for God's kingdom. God promised him, "And I will make of you *a great nation*, and *I will bless you and make your name great*,[27] so that you will be a blessing. I will bless those who bless you, and him who dishonors you I will curse, and *in you all the families of the earth shall be blessed*" (Gen. 12:2–3). Like Noah before him, Abram responded to God's command obediently, without questioning: "So Abram went, as the LORD had told him" (Gen. 12:4).

When Abram and his family "came to the land of Canaan, Abram passed through the land to the place at Shechem, to the oak of Moreh [a Canaanite shrine]. At that time the Canaanites [descendants of Canaan, whom Noah had cursed (Gen. 9:25)] were in the land. Then the LORD appeared to Abram and said, 'To your offspring I will give this land.' So he built there *an altar to the LORD*, who had appeared to him.[28] From there he moved to the hill country on the east of Bethel and pitched his tent, with Bethel on the west and Ai on the east. And there [in the center of the land] he built *an altar to the LORD* and called upon the name of the LORD" (Gen. 12:5–8). By building altars

---

27. This is in contrast to the people at Babel who had said, "Let us make a name for *ourselves*" (Gen. 11:4).

28. As Noah had done on the flood-cleansed earth (Gen. 8:20).

to the Lord next to Canaanite shrines (also in the south at Hebron by the oaks of Mamre, Gen. 13:18), Abram was reclaiming the land of Canaan for the Lord. We could, therefore, formulate the theme of this text as follows: *The Lord gave Abram/Israel—the seed of the woman— the land of the cursed Canaanites to reclaim it for the kingdom of God in order to be a blessing to all nations.*[29]

A good way to move to Jesus Christ in the New Testament is a combination of redemptive-historical progression and promise-fulfillment supported by New Testament references. By building altars to the Lord, Abram was the first to reclaim the Promised Land for God's kingdom. After their sojourn in Egypt, Israel also had to reclaim the land of the Canaanites for God's kingdom. The nation had to demonstrate the peace and justice of God's kingdom—not just for itself but as "a light for the nations."[30] When Israel failed to reflect God's kingdom of orderly cosmos, God banished them from the Promised Land.

In the fullness of time God sent his Son to restore his kingdom on earth. Jesus died for "the sins [chaos] of the whole world" (1 John 2:2) and rose from the dead [chaos to cosmos]. Then Jesus mandated his followers, "Go therefore and make disciples of *all nations*, baptizing them in the name of the Father and of the Son and of the Holy Spirit, teaching them to observe all that I have commanded you. And behold, I am with you always, to the end of the age" (Matt. 28:19–20).[31] Later Paul and Barnabas explained their mission: "For so the Lord has commanded us, saying, 'I have made you a light for the Gentiles, that you may bring *salvation to the ends of the earth*'" (Acts 13:47).

---

29. If one selects as one's preaching text the subunit Genesis 12:1–3, a good theme would be: *The Lord separates Abram from the nations in order eventually to bless the nations.*

30. See Isaiah 49:6: "I will make you as a light for the nations, that my salvation may reach to the end of the earth."

31. See Jesus's words in Matthew 24:14: "And this gospel of the kingdom will be proclaimed throughout the whole world as a testimony to *all nations*, and then the end will come."

The book of Revelation shows the final outcome. John saw in heaven "a great multitude that no one could number, *from every nation, from all tribes and peoples and languages*, standing before the throne and before the Lamb" (Rev. 7:9). Later he "saw the holy city, new Jerusalem, coming down out of heaven from God." And he "heard a loud voice from the throne saying, 'Behold, the dwelling place of God is with man. He will dwell with them, and *they will be his people, and God himself will be with them as their God*. He will wipe away every tear from their eyes, and death shall be no more, neither shall there be mourning, nor crying, nor pain anymore, for the former things have passed away'" (Rev. 21:2–4). Every form of chaos will be removed in the new Jerusalem and only orderly cosmos will remain.

John adds: "And the city has no need of sun or moon to shine on it, for the glory of God gives it light, and its lamp is the Lamb. *By its light will the nations walk, and the kings of the earth will bring their glory into it*, and its gates will never be shut by day—and there will be no night [chaos] there. They will bring into it the glory and the honor of *the nations*. But nothing unclean [chaos] will ever enter it, nor anyone who does what is detestable or false [chaos], but only those who are written in the Lamb's book of life" (Rev. 21:23–27).

In his final chapter John reveals that the new Jerusalem will be like Paradise on earth: "Then the angel showed me *the river of the water of life*, bright as crystal, flowing from the throne of God and of the Lamb through the middle of the street of the city; also, on either side of the river, *the tree of life* with its twelve kinds of fruit, yielding its fruit each month. The leaves of the tree were for *the healing of the nations* [cosmos]. No longer will there be anything accursed [chaos], but the throne of God and of the Lamb will be in it, and his servants will worship him" (Rev. 22:1–3). God and the Lamb will restore orderly cosmos on earth.

A Sermon or Lesson on Exodus 14

"God Saves Israel from the Chaotic Sea"

So far we have seen that God is sovereign over chaos and can use various forms of chaos to promote his plan for ultimate cosmos. In Exodus 14 we meet two other forms of chaos: Israel's enslavement in Egypt and the Red Sea.

The Pharaoh who did not know Joseph had enslaved Israel, ordered their baby boys to be drowned in the Nile River, and refused to let Israel go—chaos for Israel. Finally, after ten chaotic plagues, Pharaoh agreed to let Israel go. But he changed his mind when he supposed that Israel was lost in the wilderness. Pharaoh and his army pursued Israel and "overtook them encamped at the *sea*" (Ex. 14:9). The Israelites complained bitterly to the Lord and Moses, "It would have been better for us to serve the Egyptians than to die in the wilderness" (Ex. 14:12). But Moses said to them, "The Lord will fight for you, and you have only to be silent" (Ex. 14:14).

Pharaoh's armies were behind and the chaotic sea in front. Would the sea defeat Israel on its march to freedom in the Promised Land? The Lord told Moses what to do.

> Moses stretched out his hand over the sea, and *the Lord drove the sea back by a strong east wind all night and made the sea dry land*, and the waters were divided. And the people of Israel went *into the midst of the sea on dry ground*, the waters being a wall to them on their right hand and on their left. The Egyptians pursued and went in after them into the midst of the sea, all Pharaoh's horses, his chariots, and his horsemen. . . . Then the Lord said to Moses, "Stretch out

your hand over the sea, that the water may come back upon the Egyptians, upon their chariots, and upon their horsemen." So Moses stretched out his hand over the sea, and the sea returned to its normal course when the morning appeared. . . . The waters returned and covered the chariots and the horsemen; of all the host of Pharaoh that had followed them into the sea, *not one of them remained.* But the people of Israel walked on dry ground through the sea, the waters being a wall to them on their right hand and on their left. (Ex. 14:21–23, 26–29)

As with the flood, the Lord saved his people from the chaotic waters and used the same waters to swallow up those who defied him. The Lord again showed himself to be sovereign over the chaotic waters. We can, therefore, formulate the theme of this passage as follows: *While destroying his enemies with the chaotic sea, the sovereign Lord saves his people.*

A good way to move to Jesus in the New Testament is the way of analogy supported by New Testament references. As the sovereign Lord saved his people Israel from a chaotic sea, so Jesus saved his disciples from a chaotic sea.

It happened one evening when Jesus and his disciples were crossing Lake Galilee in a small boat. Suddenly a great storm arose, whipping up the waters. The mighty waves crashed into the boat and filled it with water (chaos). The disciples, who were experienced fishermen, were terrified. They woke Jesus, who was asleep in the stern, and shouted at him, "Teacher, do you not care that we are perishing [succumbing to chaos]?" Jesus "awoke and *rebuked* the wind, and said to the sea, 'Peace! Be still!' And the wind ceased, and there was a great calm [cosmos]" (Mark 4:38–39).

Jesus "rebuked the wind." The word *rebuke* is also used in Psalm 104, where the sovereign Lord rebuked the waters in the beginning when he created the earth:

> He set the earth on its foundations,
>> so that it should never be moved.
> You covered it with the deep (*tĕhôm*) as with a garment;
>> the waters (*māyim*) stood above the mountains.
> At your *rebuke* they fled;[32]
>> at the sound of your thunder they took to flight.
>> (vv. 5–7)

The word *rebuke* is also used in Psalm 106:9–10, which recalls that the Lord rebuked the Red Sea to save his people:

> He *rebuked* the Red Sea, and it became dry,
>> and he led them through the deep (*tĕhômôt*) as through
>> a desert.
> So he *saved them* from the hand of the foe
>> and redeemed them from the power of the enemy.

In the "great calm" that followed Jesus's rebuke of the wind and the sea, Jesus turned to his disciples. "He said to them, 'Why are you so afraid? Have you still no faith?' And they were filled with great fear and said to one another, 'Who then is this, that even the wind and the sea obey him?'" (Mark 4:40–41).

Who then is Jesus? With his rebuke Jesus can turn a stormy sea into a calm sea, just like the sovereign Creator God with his rebuke in the beginning turned chaos into orderly cosmos. Jesus is truly God. Who then is Jesus? Jesus can rebuke the sea to save his disciples, just

---

32. "The Greek verb translated 'rebuked' (*epitimaō*) is cognate with the noun 'rebuke' (*epitimēsis*) that is used in Psalm 104:7 (103:7 LXX) to describe the action of the divine King in quelling the chaotic sea at the time of Creation. Jesus is the divine King." Futato, *Interpreting the Psalms*, 180.

like the sovereign Lord saved Israel from the Red Sea. Jesus is Savior. He can turn chaos into cosmos, immanent death into life. His name is *Jesus*, "Yahweh saves."

An angel of the Lord told Joseph about Mary, "She will bear a son, and you shall call his name *Jesus, for he will save his people from their sins*" (Matt. 1:21). Salvation from sins (chaos) means restoration to cosmos. After Pentecost Peter and John proclaimed, "There is *salvation* in no one else, for there is *no other name* under heaven given among men by which we must be *saved*" (Acts 4:12).

There is a clear analogy between God saving Israel from the Red Sea and Jesus saving his disciples from the sea and his people from the chaos of sin. But is there also an analogy between God punishing the Egyptians in the Red Sea and Jesus punishing his enemies with chaos? Indeed there is. During his ministry on earth, Jesus already declared the woes of impending destruction: "But *woe to you*, scribes and Pharisees, hypocrites! For you shut the kingdom of heaven in people's faces. For you neither enter yourselves nor allow those who would enter to go in. . . . *Woe to you*, scribes and Pharisees, hypocrites! For you tithe mint and dill and cumin, and have neglected the weightier matters of the law: justice and mercy and faithfulness. These you ought to have done, without neglecting the others. . . . You serpents, you brood of vipers, *how are you to escape being sentenced to hell* [ultimate chaos]?" (Matt. 23:13, 23, 33).

Jesus warned, "I tell you, many will come from east and west and recline at table with Abraham, Isaac, and Jacob in the *kingdom of heaven* [cosmos], while the sons of the kingdom will be thrown into the *outer darkness*. In that place there will be weeping and gnashing of teeth" (Matt. 8:11–12). The "outer darkness" is the ultimate form of chaos.[33]

---

33. See also Jesus's parables in Matthew 22: "Bind him hand and foot and cast him into the outer darkness" (v. 13) and Matthew 25: "Cast the worthless servant into the outer darkness" (v. 30).

Jesus also spoke of the final judgment in which *Jesus* will be the judge:[34]

> When *the Son of Man* comes in his glory, and all the angels with him, then he will sit on his glorious throne. Before him will be gathered *all the nations*, and he will separate people one from another as a shepherd separates the sheep from the goats. And he will place the sheep on his right, but the goats on the left. Then the King will say to those on his right, "Come, you who are blessed by my Father, *inherit the kingdom prepared for you from the foundation of the world*. For I was hungry and you gave me food, I was thirsty and you gave me drink." . . . Then he will say to those on his left, "*Depart from me, you cursed, into the eternal fire prepared for the devil and his angels*." (Matt. 25:31–35, 41)

As the Lord punished his enemies with the chaos of the Red Sea, so in the final judgment Jesus will punish his enemies with the chaos of hell. But also, as the Lord saved Israel from the chaos of the Red Sea, so Jesus will save his people from the chaos of hell. His name, after all, is *Jesus, Joshua*, that is, "Yahweh saves." He came to restore orderly cosmos on earth.

---

34. Jesus said, "*The Father judges no one, but has given all judgment to the Son. . . .* And he has given him authority to execute judgment, because he is the Son of Man. Do not marvel at this, for an hour is coming when all who are in the tombs will hear his voice and come out, those who have done good to the resurrection of life, and those who have done evil to the *resurrection of judgment*" (John 5:22, 27–29). Paul wrote, "For we must all appear before the judgment seat *of Christ*, so that each one may receive what is due for what he has done in the body, whether good or evil" (2 Cor. 5:10).

Appendix

Reading Assignments for Bible Study Groups

It would be beneficial if all members of the study group would prepare for the discussions by studying the assigned pages of this book, reading the assigned Bible passage(s), and reflecting on and responding to the Questions for Reflection. During group discussion, feel free to skip over some questions and add others in order to focus on those issues which will provide the most helpful discussions for your particular group.

Although small groups can use this book any time for their Bible studies, ideally the discussions should take place after the pastor has preached on the fourteen passages suggested earlier (pp. 176–78).

1. Chaos–Cosmos in the Ancient Near Eastern World
Read pages 17–26.
Genesis 1:1–2:3

2. Chaos–Cosmos in Genesis
Read pages 27–44.
Genesis 3:1–24; 7:11–8:5

3. Chaos–Cosmos in Exodus and Joshua

Read pages 45–54.

Exodus 7:8–13; 14:1–15:21

4. Chaos–Cosmos in Proverbs and Job

Read pages 55–65.

Job 1:1–3:10

5. Chaos–Cosmos in Psalms

Read pages 66–80.

Psalms 2; 93; 104:1–13, 24–26; 148

6. Chaos–Cosmos in Isaiah

Read pages 81–94.

Isaiah 11:1–9; 25:7–8; 65:17–25

7. Chaos–Cosmos in Jeremiah and Ezekiel

Read pages 95–106.

Jeremiah 4:5–31; Ezekiel 47:1–12

8. Chaos–Cosmos in the Minor Prophets

Read pages 107–15.

Joel 2:1–11, 30–31; Zechariah 3:1–10

9. Chaos–Cosmos in Daniel

Read pages 116–20.

Daniel 7:1–14; 12:1–4

10. Chaos–Cosmos in the Gospels

Read pages 121–34.

Mark 15:33–16:8

11. Chaos–Cosmos in Acts

Read pages 135–39.

Acts 2:1–47

12. Chaos–Cosmos in the Epistles

Read pages 140–50.
Colossians 1:9–20

13. Chaos–Cosmos in Revelation 1–19

Read pages 151–62.
Revelation 1:1–20

14. Chaos–Cosmos in Revelation 20–22

Read pages 163–73.
Revelation 21:1–27

Selected Bibliography

Books and articles not listed in this select bibliography have full publication details in their first listing in the footnotes and in shorter form thereafter.

Anderson, Bernhard W. *Creation Versus Chaos: The Reinterpretation of Mythical Symbolism in the Bible*. New York: Association Press, 1967.

———. *From Creation to New Creation: Old Testament Perspectives*. Minneapolis, MN: Fortress, 1994.

Beale, Gregory K. *A New Testament Biblical Theology: The Unfolding of the Old Testament in the New*. Grand Rapids, MI: Baker, 2011.

Brueggemann, Walter. *Theology of the Old Testament: Testimony, Dispute, Advocacy*. Minneapolis, MN: Fortress, 1997.

———. "The Book of Exodus." In *The New Interpreter's Bible*, vol. 1. Nashville: Abingdon, 1994.

Childs, Brevard. *Myth and Reality in the Old Testament*. London: SCM, 1960.

Cohn, Norman. *Cosmos, Chaos and the World to Come: The Ancient Roots of Apocalyptic Faith*. New Haven, CT: Yale University Press, 1993.

Collins, Adela Yarbro. *The Combat Myth in the Book of Revelation*. Missoula, MT: Scholars Press, 1976.

Davidson, Richard M. "The Genesis Account of Origins." In *The Genesis Creation Account and Its Reverberations in the Old Testament*. Edited by Gerald A. Klingbeil. Berrien Springs, MI: Andrews University Press, 2015, 59–148.

———. "The Creation Theme in Psalm 104." In *The Genesis Creation Account and Its Reverberations in the Old Testament*. Edited by Gerald A. Klingbeil. Berrien Springs, MI: Andrews University Press, 2015, 149–88.

Davidson, Robert. *The Vitality of Worship: A Commentary on the Book of Psalms*. Grand Rapids, MI: Eerdmans, 1998.

Day, John N. *God's Conflict with the Dragon and the Sea: Echoes of a Canaanite Myth in the Old Testament*. Cambridge: Cambridge University Press, 1985.

Deroche, Michael. "Isaiah 45:7 and the Creation of Chaos." *VT* 42, no. 1 (1992): 11–21.

Fretheim, Terence E. *God and World in the Old Testament: A Relational Theology of Creation*. Nashville: Abingdon, 2005.

———. *Creation Untamed: The Bible, God, and Natural Disasters*. Grand Rapids, MI: Baker, 2010.

Frymer-Kensky, Tikva. "The Atrahasis Epic and Its Significance for Our Understanding of Genesis 1–9." *BA* 40 (1974): 147–55.

Futato, Mark David. *Interpreting the Psalms: An Exegetical Handbook*. Grand Rapids, MI: Kregel, 2007.

Greidanus, Sidney. *Preaching Christ from Genesis: Foundations for Expository Sermons*. Grand Rapids, MI: Eerdmans, 2007.

———. *Preaching Christ from Daniel: Foundations for Expository Sermons*. Grand Rapids, MI: Eerdmans, 2012.

———. *Preaching Christ from Psalms: Foundations for Expository Sermons in the Christian Year*. Grand Rapids, MI: Eerdmans, 2016.

Hasel, Gerhard and Michael, "The Unique Cosmology of Genesis 1 against Ancient Near Eastern and Egyptian Parallels." In *The Genesis Creation Account and Its Reverberations in the Old Testament*. Edited by Gerald A. Klingbeil. Berrien Springs, MI: Andrews University Press, 2015, 9–29.

Hoekema, Anthony A. *The Bible and the Future*. Grand Rapids, MI: Eerdmans, 1979.

Hubbard, Robert L., Jr. "The Spirit and Creation." In *Presence, Power, and Promise: The Role of the Spirit of God in the Old Testament*. Edited by David G. Firth and Paul D. Wegner. Downers Grove, IL: InterVarsity Press, 2011, 71–91.

Kidner, Derek. *Genesis*. Chicago: InterVarsity Press, 1967.

Kraus, Hans Joachim. *Psalms 60–150: A Continental Commentary*. Translated by Hilton C. Oswald. Minneapolis, MN: Fortress, 1993.

Leder, Arie C. "Hearing Exodus 7:8–13 to Preach the Gospel: The Ancient Adversary in Today's World." *CTJ* 43, no. 1 (2008): 93–110.

Mays, James Luther. *Psalms*. Louisville, KY: John Knox, 1994.

Mellish, Kevin. "Creation as Social and Political Order in Ancient Thought and the Hebrew Bible." *WeslTJ* 44, no. 1 (2009): 157–79.

Miller, Patrick D. *Interpreting the Psalms*. Philadelphia: Fortress, 1986.

Niditch, Susan. *Chaos to Cosmos: Studies in Biblical Patterns of Creation*. Chico, CA: Scholars Press, 1985.

NIV Study Bible. Grand Rapids, MI: Zondervan, 1985.

Routledge, Robin. "Did God Create Chaos?: Unresolved Tension in Genesis 1:1–2." *TynBul* 61, no. 1 (2010): 69–88.

Sarna, Nahum M. *On the Book of Psalms: Exploring the Prayers of Ancient Israel*. New York: Schocken, 1993.

Stek, John. *NIV Study Bible*, "Psalms" Introduction and Notes. Grand Rapids, MI: Zondervan, 1985.

Tsumura, David Toshio. *Creation and Destruction: A Reappraisal of the Chaoskampf Theory in the Old Testament*. Winona Lake, IN: Eisenbrauns, 2005.

Vail, Eric M. *Creation and Chaos Talk: Charting a Way Forward*. Eugene, OR: Pickwick, 2012.

von Rad, Gerhard. *Genesis: A Commentary*. Philadelphia: Westminster, 1972.

Wallace, Howard. "Leviathan and the Beast in Revelation." *BA*, 11 (1948): 61–68.

Waltke, Bruce K. "The Creation Account in Genesis 1:1–3." *BSac* 132, no. 525 (1975): 25–36; no. 526 (1975): 136–44; no. 527 (1975): 216–28; no. 528 (1975): 327–42; 133 no. 529 (1976): 28–41.

———. *Genesis: A Commentary*. Grand Rapids, MI: Zondervan, 2001.

Walton, John H. "Creation in Genesis 1:1–2:3 and the Ancient Near East: Order out of Disorder after Chaoskampf." *CTJ* 43 (2008): 48–63.

———. *Genesis 1 as Ancient Cosmology*. Winona Lake, IN: Eisenbrauns, 2011.

Watson, Rebecca S. *Chaos Uncreated: The Reassessment of the Theme of "Chaos" in the Hebrew Bible*. Berlin, Germany: Walter de Gruyter, 2005.

Wenham, Gordon J. *Genesis 1–15*. Waco, TX: Word Books, 1987.

General Index

Selected Scripture Index

Short Studies in Biblical
Theology Series

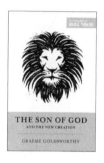

THE SON OF GOD
AND THE NEW CREATION

GRAEME GOLDSWORTHY

MARRIAGE
AND THE MYSTERY OF THE GOSPEL

RAY ORTLUND

WORK
AND OUR LABOR IN THE LORD

JAMES M. HAMILTON JR.

COVENANT
AND GOD'S PURPOSE FOR THE WORLD

THOMAS R. SCHREINER

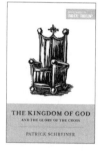

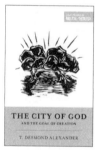

THE KINGDOM OF GOD
AND THE GLORY OF THE CROSS

PATRICK SCHREINER

THE CITY OF GOD
AND THE GOAL OF CREATION

T. DESMOND ALEXANDER

FROM CHAOS TO COSMOS
CREATION TO NEW CREATION

SIDNEY GREIDANUS

For more information, visit **crossway.org/ssbt**.